Success Unleashed

Success Unleashed

Mastering Your Life's Purpose

by
JP Bachmann

Table of Contents

Preface

You are special. You are unique. You have worth. You have something to bring to this world that no one else can offer, and it's up to you to discover exactly what that is.

The goal of this book is to help you realize and unlock your life's potential. Over the years, I have observed thousands of people who appear to be drifting through life without any specific purpose or direction. I've now reached a point in my life that I understand my purpose. As I look back, even at my own occasions when I've drifted, I can't help but wonder why more people don't understand *why* they exist.

This book is not directed to a Christian audience, but it has been written from a Christian worldview. I believe there is a God who created every individual on the planet, and in that creation has had a specific and unique purpose for each of us.

"The two most important days of your life are the day you were born and the day you find out why." This quote has generally been attributed to Mark Twain, though there is some

question about the quote's actual origin. From my perspective, the latter part of that statement is what most people are typically seeking. Regardless of whether you subscribe to religious beliefs, the fact that you've picked up this book suggests you understand there is more to life than what you currently experience—and you'd like to understand what that is.

Within these pages, you will find stories from people I have interacted with during the past few years as well as some of my own stories. Their names have been changed to protect their identities. I have learned much about different cultures, thought processes and circumstances from each of these people. I have chosen to be very open and vulnerable in describing my personal stories. It was my intention to allow the readers to understand that we may have shared experiences. Through these stories and experiences, I hope you will be able to overcome challenges you may have in your life so that you can reach your full potential.

To understand why you were born, you must understand where you've come from. You must understand your own mental wiring and break the bonds which hold you in the position you are in today. This is the most difficult part of everyone's journey. One of the most critical things to understand is that there are other people out there just like you who have broken those bonds in their lives. This means that *you can, too!*

Throughout this book we'll cover some sensitive topics. The goal is to expose areas within your life that may be holding you back without you realizing it. The sooner you can identify and address these areas, the faster you will be on the road to success.

To fully appreciate the content of this book, it's important to define what success is and what it is not. When people think of success, they often think about money or possessions. While these can be indicators of some success, it's really an incomplete definition. If your goal is to live in a certain location or to have a certain amount of money set aside for retirement, you will easily be able to realize when you've reached that specific goal. However, not all success is tangible.

In the context of this book, success refers to the completion of a specific goal or the realization of your purpose. Or both. It may be something tangible like wealth or possessions. It could be how you look, feel or are treated by others. Maybe it's what you are able to accomplish within your community, having a nice job title or the ability to start a business or grow your company to a certain size. Success is not defined by anyone other than you, and the realization of that success is entirely yours.

Does this mean success doesn't involve other people? Of course not! What you'll discover throughout this book is that other people must be a part of your success journey. Some will function as accountability partners to keep you on track *(see Chapter 4)*. Others will be companions who can help you avoid the pain of going through the process alone. They may also be mentors or coaches who will help you unlock ideas or educate you in highly specified areas, enabling you to reach the next stage of your success journey faster than you could have on your own.

My original intent was to focus on success and how to achieve it; however, during the writing process I discovered a much deeper outcome it could help you achieve. In examining my own goal, I came to the realization that the application of principles within these pages could enable someone to answer one of life's deepest questions: Why am I here?

No, I'm not claiming this book reveals the meaning of life; but I have found that when these methods are applied regularly and examined deeply enough, you can discover the meaning of *your* life. You, dear reader, were designed to do something unique and amazing. You have a purpose, and I hope you experience even a fraction of the excitement I did when I discovered this for myself.

How to Use This Book
Personal development books come in different varieties. Some are meant to grow your intellectual knowledge or shift your thinking on a particular topic. Some are designed for you to actively engage or to go through exercises to develop specific skills. This book is intended to do both.

The first five chapters are informative in nature. You will understand the power that certain aspects of the world have within our lives. The remaining chapters contain additional information and personal stories. They also require some form of action on your part. A supplemental worksheet may be downloaded for free at www.thedashlegacy.net/downloads. This will help you work through each of the described methods. The worksheet can be used to describe your goals and dig into them, fully understanding them. The more goals you establish by using the method outlined in this book, the more likely you will be able to discover a pattern which can help you pinpoint your life's purpose.

The chapter on abuse was difficult for me to write because there are many books on this subject already. This is not exhaustive by any means, and is in place to provide several examples that could possibly cause difficulty for some readers in fully embracing the methods and habits discussed. As you read that section, you may realize that you have past issues that have not yet been dealt with and should be, or you may have had challenges that are not addressed. Regardless, the understanding that trauma and abuse exist to the degrees that they do may help you move forward, or may even provide you with empathy for those around you who struggle in unseen ways.

Throughout the book you will see references to the BIAS (Build, Imagine, Act & Say Yes) mindset and WISE (Write, Imagine, Specify, Evangelize) goalsetting methodology. These are described in detail in the second half and are the crux of what will be taught. To discover your life's purpose and develop the habits that will achieve success in all you do, you will be able to see, feel, taste, smell and hear your future. That might sound strange, but when properly applied these methods will work in ways you may not be able to imagine today.

Perhaps you don't currently have the right people in your life who can help get you to where you need to be. You will learn how to better develop a network of people who can push and/or pull you in the right directions. Our organization also partners with a team of business and life coaches whom you can hire to fill gaps within your own network until your support system can thrive effectively.

Be sure to share your feedback. Tell your story about how you used the BIAS Mindset to find your internal greatness.

Send us a comment at www.thedashlegacy.net about how this system has worked for you, or feel free to tell us your story so we can reach new audiences. Become a part of this story and help us improve the lives of others throughout our community.

Good luck as you embark on this journey! It's going to take time, and it's worth every second. You will become the best version of yourself by applying the BIAS Mindset, and I can't wait to hear your story.

Chapter 1
The Standard

"[The caste system][1] is the worn grooves of comforting routines and unthinking expectations, patterns of a social order that have been in place for so long that it looks like the natural order of things."

—Isabel Wilkerson
Caste: The Origins of Our Discontents

In the United States, we live in a caste system. When this idea occurred to me, my first thought was *no way*. From an economic and political perspective, ours does not compare to India's and Nepal's. For example, they believe the community in which someone is born into is their lot for life. However, a degree of caste within our society can be described best as a self-imposed caste based on our backgrounds, socio-economic status, income or education.

If you look within the structure of our society, you will

---

1   www.goodreads.com/work/quotes/75937597-caste-the-origins-of-our-discontents

find elite billionaire business owners, political elite, celebrities, corporate executives and investors who all exist within the top levels of our caste hierarchy. This level of achievement is often a big jump from the broad middle class. The upper middle class includes most levels of management, some of our military, many of our educated government workers, and some high-achieving individual contributors. The lower-middle class and low-income caste are largely uneducated and "down in the trenches" when it comes to their daily jobs. Our poor, who range from homeless to living in subsidized housing, are often on welfare and food stamps, and they scramble for basic necessities. They have very few opportunities to climb the economic ladder.

Most of us have heard stories of people who have raised themselves from rags to riches or who got lucky through an inheritance, a good investment or a big windfall such as the lottery. However, these are outlying scenarios and are not accepted as believable or realistic for nearly everyone else.

People want to change their lives so much that they will line up to buy lottery tickets every single week despite the incredibly low odds of experiencing windfalls. This would suggest that people believe they aren't able to achieve their dreams, live the life they hope for or break free from the bondage of their American caste.

Many people who experience a sudden windfall often end up bankrupt within a few years because of the inability to deal with newfound wealth. Rags-to-riches stories are the result of something that is typically done once, such as creating an invention or developing a unique business within the overall market.

Are you ready for the good news? You are not stuck in this caste system! You are free to achieve success, and nothing in the world is stopping you. Your past does not define your future. Where you are in life today does not mean that tomorrow, or in a few short years, you can't be in an entirely different place.

What will make the biggest difference is what rests between your ears. How you condition your mind will ultimately determine your ability to rise above the caste you are currently in. You can achieve greatness, because inside of you right now is a specific talent or passion capable of keeping you up at night. The purpose you were born with can drive you into your future and allow you to be better than anyone else on the planet.

For most of my life, I have not been what others might call successful. I did not believe in myself, and I didn't think I was allowed to be successful. Why did I have these doubts? Many things I do now result in success. I have worked hard to hone my abilities. I have been so close to my purpose for years without realizing it, and the passion behind that purpose has allowed me to achieve much of what I set out to do. But before I tell you what changed, I need to start from the beginning.

I grew up in a small agricultural community in southern Washington state. My family wasn't originally from the west coast. In fact, I was born on the east coast near the Atlantic Ocean. My parents made the decision when I was very young to uproot our family, leaving behind all that we knew to travel nearly 3,000 miles away. We didn't know anyone near our new home, and we had to make a new name for ourselves. A large part of this decision was based on deep-rooted family issues, and my parents just needed to get away. Another driving factor was that there were new opportunities out west, and my father wanted to take advantage of them. He had always been a highly independent thinker with an incredible work ethic and a grit we rarely see today.

Neither of my parents were educated beyond high school. Except for an uncle on my mother's side, no one in my family had ever received a college education. Despite the new opportunities my parents sought out, they never rose above the base level within their career fields.

There was one major issue that kept my parents from achieving a high level of success. It wasn't their education, and it definitely wasn't their work ethic. Both of them could work circles around their peers and had incredible attention to detail in their work. What kept them from moving into higher and more equitable positions was their mindset. I'll focus here on my father, because he influenced much of my mentality in the early years of my life.

My father did not grow up in what we would now call a healthy living environment. The neighborhood was rough, often placing him in physical danger. His parents were not very supportive. His mother regarded children as burdens; and for the first nine years of my father's life, he was the only child. When a sibling finally came along, my father had already been relegated to the "bad son" role and was treated accordingly. He suffered much verbal and physical abuse and was often neglected.

When he finished high school, he was given a chance to go to college. Knowing that option would have kept him attached to his parents, he opted to enlist in the United States

Navy during the Vietnam conflict so he could separate himself from the abuse he had been subjected to.

In Vietnam, my father witnessed even more tragedy and trauma. The poor leadership managing the war led to much risk and hardship. His military base was overrun multiple times while he was in country, and there was not enough fighting equipment available to issue to everyone who wasn't on duty. During the times the base was overrun while he was off duty, my father had to find a place to hide since he couldn't get a rifle to fight back with. This resulted in even more distrust of authority figures.

The distrust of leadership followed him for the rest of his life. Because of his defiant behavior toward them, they in turn did not trust him. It became a horrible feedback loop throughout his career.

Though my father was an extremely dedicated and hard worker, I had always heard stories while growing up about how bad leadership was. "*The suits in their ivory towers are barking orders. They'll tell us what to do, but they don't have any idea how to do it themselves.*" The people in leadership were portrayed to me as evil, greedy people who didn't have any value.

My father's opinion about leadership and the way he fought with them about everything was his undoing. He didn't see the value in climbing the corporate ladder. Because of his attitude he was never offered positions that could have made life so much better for his family.

Hearing stories like this when I was growing up made an impression in my life. I didn't want to grow up to be evil or greedy. I wanted to make sure whatever I did had value. I grew up doing chores and learning the work ethic my father exhibited. I never aspired to do anything more with my life than he had done with his.

How we are raised makes a huge impression on us. I have come to the pivotal realization that what I grew up believing as truth was nothing more than a glass prison where I held myself prisoner. I was fortunate to have found a few mentors who helped dispel those lies so I could shatter the glass and move forward in my life.

I recently had dinner with a woman I'll call Tanya. When I heard her story, I started to feel better about the conditions in which I grew up. My family was not well off by any means, but she had grown up in extreme poverty.

Tanya was one of seven children who grew up in the low-income region of her city. They had a roof over their heads, but there wasn't much else. Her father was serving an extended prison term, and her mother had to rely on food stamps to put basics on the table. Those would usually run out about halfway through the month. There were very few ways (other than gambling or theft) to earn enough money to put food on the table. During the cold of winter, the electricity was off more than it was on, and they stole firewood from their neighbors just to keep warm as they bundled and huddled together in their dark, frozen house.

As Tanya's siblings reached adulthood, they were all in and out of jail. Most had felonies, and the bullying of Tanya continued since she was able to keep herself on the right side of the law. Because her siblings maintained their generational caste, Tanya's choice to take a different path caused additional strife within her family.

    Success Unleashed: Mastering Your Life's Purpose

Tanya knew there had to be more to life than the extremes of cold and hunger. She attended school as often as possible despite her family's contempt at her desire to get an education. Her mother would often pull her out of school to make her collect food stamps, buy groceries and do the cooking and cleaning in the home. She thought this was incredibly unfair because this requirement was never applied to her brothers and sisters. Tanya was the oldest girl in the family, so her mother saw this as her responsibility. The rest of the kids could destroy the house and slack off all they wanted while she earned all the punishment for their misdeeds.

Despite all this, Tanya persisted in her desire to get an education. She lacked the basic supplies to do her schoolwork; her friends would often share theirs with her so she could complete her assignments. She tried to be sociable, but it was difficult because other kids would avoid her. She was usually unwashed, and her clothes were threadbare or had holes in them. Even the soles of her shoes were falling off.

She still struggles with habits and tendencies that were set deeply within her from childhood. She struggles with trusting others. She hoards things most people would take for granted, such as sheets of paper or pens and pencils. She associates with drug addicts and felons. These habits have resulted in difficulty with jobs, lawyers and healthy friendships. She had made the decision to not have any children of her own when she became an adult because of how poorly she was treated. She didn't want that trend to continue, so she sacrificed that part of her life to stop the trend.

Tanya had faced so many hardships, but there were people who came into her life who delivered just enough hope to allow her to continue. Her third-grade teacher was one such person. Because Tanya didn't have the basic supplies to do her schoolwork, her teacher would always find ways to get Tanya what she needed. She would have her stay back from recess to help with something in the classroom. When Tanya finished a task, she would be rewarded by being allowed to choose an item from a box. There was always something in the box that would enable her to continue—pencils, erasers, protractors, etc.

That experience was one of the most impactful moments in Tanya's life. Someone else was willing to give her what she needed with no expectation of anything in return. This lesson has stuck with Tanya as strongly as the feeling of cold, dark nights with her family huddled in the living room of their house. She now works with various youth programs; and because of her own experience, she is able to identify children who live in similar conditions that she grew up in. Her mission is to make sure that underprivileged kids are seen and encouraged in a way no one else can or will.

Not all success will result in riches. Tanya is a success because she has found her purpose. She was able to use her own broken experience as a child to help make a better world for children who grow up in similar circumstances. Her purpose is to see and hear those who do not have a voice. Her ability to reach into those lives is helping to ease those children out of poverty, which helps them work through depression and any suicidal tendencies they may be experiencing. Her gift to the world is the ability to show love to the unlovable and help them to rise above their caste.

Not all stories are born in tragedy. Some people have

    Success Unleashed: Mastering Your Life's Purpose

more normal upbringings (if there is such a thing). "Andrei" was born in Romania and immigrated to the United States with his family when he was 6 years old. His father was a successful electrical engineer and was able to bring his training with him to the US. Andrei and his siblings were encouraged to experiment, and they learned what captured their interest. Unlike most in the Information Technology career field, college was not part of the discussion.

Because of his father's engineer training, Andrei was exposed to electrical theory at a very young age. He also had a knack for engineering and built his first computer by the age of 8. He started his own business at age 10 by building computers in the garage and selling them to his friends and neighbors. He would use the profits to buy the things he wanted, such as a new bike or better computer equipment.

Andrei didn't pursue college because the new family business allowed him to use skills he had developed to take care of people's technical needs. Early into his adulthood, Andrei sought a job where he could learn in a more formal environment. He quickly advanced into a leadership role because of his curiosity and willingness to learn.

Andrei is unique in his career field. He has excelled because of grit, which has earned him promotions much faster than his peers. He and his wife have chosen to take different roles in their respective careers. This has allowed them to move to different states and gain new perspectives and opportunities. Because of his attitude, curiosity and work ethic, Andrei achieved the executive position of Chief Information Security Officer at two companies by his mid-30s.

Romania is the second poorest country in the European

Union. They were under communist rule until the late 1980s, and there were few opportunities to expand one's career prospects while living there. By moving to the United States, Andrei's family could have reasonably expected a similar life when they arrived in the US. They could have continued with their similar Romanian lifestyle, but they refused to accept that as an option. His parents opened a family business and began teaching their children how to be entrepreneurs.

Several of Andrei's older brothers and sisters chose to squander their opportunities. They turned their backs on their church and family which resulted in divorce and struggle. Andrei wouldn't accept that as his fate and chose to rise above. He pursued knowledge and fostered his own curiosity rather than formally studying for a college degree. He leaned into the family business with grit and determination that would ultimately make him wildly successful.

Andrei did not choose to sit on his hands and get caught in the same patterns demonstrated by his peers. Instead, he made the conscious decision to always push forward. He demonstrated a BIAS mindset which has launched him into an executive-level career within two decades of his very first job.

Remember that your history does not limit you. The conditions in which you live now need not be a permanent situation. Although Tanya still has challenges, she understands that by remaining on the good side of the law and working hard, she can not only have a fruitful life of her own but can also uplift and influence the lives of impoverished children. Andrei could have easily walked in the footsteps of his siblings, but he knew that with the right mindset he could change his family's legacy.

 Success Unleashed: Mastering Your Life's Purpose

If you want to change, you can. If you do not feel valued by those around you, understand that you do have value. You can achieve whatever you set your mind to. By following the BIAS mindset, you will change the patterns of your life, which will allow you to rebuild your family legacy based on the way you were designed. You can discover your purpose and make a lasting impact on the world around you.

Chapter 2
Abuse

"Overcoming abuse doesn't just happen; it takes positive steps every day. Let today be the day you start to move forward."

—Assunta Harris

In the pursuit of purpose or passions and in the achievement of major goals, many people have experienced lies, abuse and otherwise terrible treatment from others along the way. For many readers, this could open serious wounds from the past. In order to realize your full potential, you must understand that certain situations you have dealt with, or are currently dealing with, can hold you back. To move forward, we sometimes must correct issues from our past.

The ugly treatment you may have dealt with in your life is not your fault. Abuse and addiction are difficult subjects to parse into a single chapter, but we must acknowledge they are barriers which prevent many from truly discovering who they are destined to be. This chapter is not designed to provide healing insight; rather, it will bring to light areas that may need to be examined in greater detail.

You have a purpose for being here. My hope is that the following material will create in you the ability to realize you have worth and value. Use the examples herein to help you develop understanding and empathy for those who have experienced their own forms of abuse.

Abuse is incredibly difficult to overcome because it can alter our psyche. When people are abused, they can experience several major changes such as chronic depression, post-traumatic stress disorder, personality disorders, substance abuse, sleep issues, anxiety and even suicide. There is hope, though. People can take advantage of methods, treatments and steps to overcome whatever they've dealt with and use them to fulfill their purpose in life.

Abuse, in any form, stems from someone else's weakness. Despite the mental and physical pain to the victim, abuse is a lie presenting as truth. When someone experiences long-term abuse, the terrible situation begins to feel like normal reality. If it goes on too long, it will eventually bleed over into every area and aspect of their lives until they no longer realize it doesn't have to be that way.

Before we get into specifics, here are a few statistics to consider about different forms of abuse:

- Almost 60% of Americans surveyed say they suffered at least one form of physical or emotional abuse or other adversity in their childhoods.[2]

This means that about 3 out of every 5 people you

---

2   www.reuters.com/article/idUSTRE6BF4MZ

encounter have been exposed to or have been the victim of violence, sexual abuse, psychological abuse or another form of crime in their homes during their developmental years.

- 20.2% of students experience bullying.[3]
- Children growing up with abuse are 6 times more likely to become abusers as adults.[4]
- 55% of American workers have experienced some form of discrimination at their current company.[5]
- According to the National Library of Medicine, approximately 1 in 4 children experiences child abuse or neglect in his/her lifetime. Of maltreated children, 18% are abused physically, 78% are neglected, and 9% are abused sexually.[6]
- According to the Centers for Disease Control, 1 in 4 women and about 1 in 26 men have experienced complete or attempted rape.[7]
- In 2022, the National Survey on Drug Use and Health found that 29.5 million people ages 12 and older (10.5% in this age group) had AUD (Alcohol Use Disorder) in the past year.[8]
- The National Center for Drug Abuse Statics lists three key findings:[9]

3   www.pacer.org/bullying/info/stats.asp
4   www.ojp.gov/ncjrs/virtual-library/abstracts/do-abused-children-become-abusive-parents
5   www.nasdaq.com/articles/6-statistics-to-better-understand-the-extent-of-discrimination-in-the-workplace
6   www.ncbi.nlm.nih.gov/books/NBK470337
7   www.cdc.gov/sexual-violence/about
8   www.niaaa.nih.gov/alcohols-effects-health/alcohol-topics/alcohol-facts-and-statistics/alcohol-use-disorder-aud-united-states-age-groups-and-demographic-characteristics
9   www.drugabusestatistics.org

   Success Unleashed: Mastering Your Life's Purpose

- ° 50% of people 12 and older have used illicit drugs at least once;
- ° there have been over 700,000 drug overdose deaths in the US since 2000; and
- ° the federal budget for drug control in 2020 was $35 billion despite drugs being abused at near epidemic levels.

There is a high statistical probability that you, dear reader, are among these statistics. In many cases, those situations were completely out of your control. Those within your control could easily be a result of life's typical stresses and abuses. The substance abuse problem is amplified by the normalization of certain behaviors in our society. The media (including "unscripted" programming, sports reporting, several genres of music, movies and regular television) tend to highlight and glorify celebrities who engage in reckless behavior.

When we idolize superstars who manage their own stress through toxic outlets, it broadcasts a message to the rest of us that this type of behavior is acceptable. Some may even draw the conclusion that through these substances they will attain the same fortune and fame as the celebrities who are ruining their lives and killing themselves.

Following are descriptions of some common forms of abuse. If any of these are familiar in your life, you may wish to address those issues before moving forward to discover your passion and achieve your life-goals. At the end of this chapter you will find a few possible alternatives to consider that may help you overcome any challenges that may be holding you back from achieving success.

Physical Abuse

There is a fine line between discipline and physical abuse. The information age has allowed our society to bring to light many of the different forms of abuse throughout our culture. This is one of the few times I will ever praise social media. The result from this heightened awareness is that we've seen a decline in the severity of physical abuse in our nation. However, the problem still exists at alarming levels.

In past generations it was commonplace for a parent or grandparent to spank or discipline their children using implements. In fact, when I was growing up my parents used a belt or a wooden spoon to administer corporal punishment. The philosophy behind this method (at least in my house) was that if a parent used their hand to strike a child, that child would associate the pain with the parent rather than through a foreign object.

Another common form of punishment is the act of hitting to teach a lesson. It can range from severe spanking to slapping, punching, kicking, scratching, pushing, pulling on ears or hair, or worse. Considered by many to be discipline, this is nothing more than abuse. When parents use their superior size and strength to rationalize beating their children, it is not healthy or normal.

When people experience traumatic situations such as physical or sexual abuse, their minds become reprogrammed in a way similar to those who have experienced car accidents or military and police who have experienced combat. Our brains cannot quantify these occurrences, so we are not able to distinguish a certain event as belonging to our past. We continue to relive these situations as if they are still happening today. This is very similar to Post Traumatic Stress Disorder (PTSD). In his book, *The Body Keeps the Score*, Dr. Bessel Van Der Kolk describes the research, findings and treatment associated with this phenomenon.

Physical and emotional abuse will leave lasting scars on a person. The psychological impact can cause them to react to situations in unpredictable ways. For example, if an abuse victim experiences a difficult or stressful situation at work, he or she may physically experience that as a life-threatening event. Proper treatment can help abuse victims recategorize as a past event such triggers as these, but without it they could be stuck in a loop of aggression, anxiety or depression every time they encounter stressful events. This can have significant impacts and could eventually prevent them from moving forward toward their life or career goals.

If this describes you, encourage yourself to find out more. There are several healthy and effective methods available, and there is no shame in seeking help. Without taking this step, you may find it difficult to follow the methods discussed in later chapters.

Some readers may be in a situation where physical discipline or abuse is still present. If anyone close to you expresses deep emotions through causing pain, bruising, cutting, hitting or slapping, please understand it is not a healthy environment. You have the right to be treated with respect and physical safety. You do not deserve this kind of treatment, and it's important that you quickly find a way to remove yourself from the situation.

Many people find it difficult to remove themselves because they believe they deserve to be treated this way. *You do not deserve it!* Seek help, even through your local authorities if necessary. I do not recommend revenge or retaliation, which will likely make the situation worse. By completely removing yourself and seeking appropriate help, you will be taking the first steps toward the healthy and physically safe life you deserve.

Sexual Abuse

Nothing breaks my heart more than people who take advantage of others sexually. When people (particularly children) are subjected to sexual abuse, their minds become so warped that a normal, healthy physical relationship becomes difficult or even impossible.

A young woman confided in me about her home life during puberty. Her stepfather would regularly molest her by touching her developing chest or her pubic area. This always occurred while he was drunk. He took advantage of her innocence, and she was powerless to stop him. Her biological father was extremely abusive and had sent her mother to the emergency room several times before she was finally able to escape with her children.

The physical and sexual abuses this young woman had witnessed and experienced warped her perception of men. When she entered adulthood, she rejected the idea of having healthy relationships with men by pursuing homosexual relationships. Even today she suffers from extreme anxiety and severe depression. During several discussions with her, she has expressed to me a desire to die, though she has not exhibited suicidal tendencies.

Worse was her sister, who experienced the same sexual

abuse by their stepfather. She turned out differently, though, perhaps because she was too young to remember the physical assaults of her mother by her biological father. Rather than avoiding men, she did the opposite. She sought men for validation and acceptance and was willing to sacrifice her own body for sex so she wouldn't have to suffer the indignity of losing a boyfriend. Several of the young men she attached herself to took advantage of her, and she gave away her virginity shortly after turning 14. It was because of this need for validation from young men that she made a terrible decision to go on a joy ride with her boyfriend and another young man, which tragically resulted in a major car crash that ended her life.

It is estimated that 1 in 4 women has been a victim of an attempted or completed rape in her lifetime (14.8% completed, 2.8% completed). 90% of all rape victims are female. In 2020, there were approximately 167.5 million women in the United States, which means that nearly 28 million women had been subject to this type of assault. Adding to this challenge is that only 33% of rapes are reported to the authorities, and less than 1% of those rapes lead to a felony conviction. Due to the lack of justice applied to this heinous crime, there are few deterrents for perpetrators to stop their wretched behavior.

When girls and young women are assaulted or abused sexually, they develop a misunderstanding about their bodies and relationships, creating potential conditions like PTSD that can last for years. In extreme cases, women subjected to these horrible situations are unable to build trusting relationships with men and can sometimes react violently when approached sexually by someone they intend to have a romantic relationship with.

Boys and young men are also sexually abused. A very small percentage qualifies as rape, and it is unfortunately a widely accepted double standard in our society that men are supposed to be sexualized.[10] When developing boys and young men are over-sexualized, they fail to respect their own bodies, and their capacity to respect women is greatly diminished.

Sexual identity often contributes to many more types of attitudes and behaviors. If we fail to address this abuse as a culture and we continue to normalize sexual deviancy, the more likely we will see a continuing breakdown of our society.

Despite what extreme ideologues would have you believe, promiscuity, pornography, sexual exploration, molestation, rape and sexual assault are abnormal behaviors. Regardless of the severity or nature of the sexual assault, these are not good, healthy or normal behaviors. Being violated in a sexual manner against one's will can severely skew his/her ability to function properly in an otherwise healthy sexual relationship. This can ultimately be a limitation to finding purpose and passion or to achieving their life-goals effectively.

Unwanted/Neglected Children

Throughout history there have been cases of children being born unexpectedly such as through sexual trysts resulting in unwanted pregnancies, married couples not intending to have children, or having a child at an early or late stage in life.

If children come along unexpectedly, or if a parent is not emotionally stable enough to properly care for a child, chil-

---

10 www.ncbi.nlm.nih.gov/pmc/articles/PMC4244004

  Success Unleashed: Mastering Your Life's Purpose

dren can become the victims. In many cases, the neglect children experience can be accompanied by physical or sexual abuse, or the children can be ignored completely.

Often, those children are not provided with the basic means to support a healthy development, particularly in low-income or single-parent situations. Examples include malnourishment, worn or inappropriate clothing, lack of education, exposure to illness, lack of adequate health care and even hostile environments created by criminal activity, homelessness or drug abuse.

When children are neglected, they are unable to develop the necessary social bonds that allow them to function normally within society. They tend to resort to criminal activity like shoplifting, assault, burglary and joining gangs. They are unable to see the value of education and in some cases are forbidden by their parents or guardians from attending school at all. Some are illiterate, and many end up turning to drugs or alcohol at a very young age.

A pastor friend of mine shared a story with me about a man he had been counseling who didn't understand why he was angry all the time. In his 40s, he had finally approached his mother to find out why he was treated so differently than his siblings who were significantly younger than him. His mother told him that she never wanted him in the first place. How horrible to learn something like that so late in life! This man had grown up with the understanding that he had no value. But as with every other situation, he (like you) has value. He has a purpose in this life and the ability to achieve his dreams.

When children grow up with parents who shun their responsibility, it can create a ripple effect that lasts for generations. The children may grow up to shun their own responsibilities or treat other people with disrespect or contempt. They may even end up being negligent parents themselves. They could also develop unhealthy emotional states like the man who was counseled. For him, the inability to process situations emotionally resulted in unexplained anger and rage. For others, they might constantly seek connection in unhealthy ways such as through multiple sexual encounters, gang activity or harassment or mistreatment of those around them. In other cases, they may completely withdraw from society and isolate themselves.

Psychological Abuse

Not all abuse leaves physical evidence. In the cases above, the abuse can often be seen through bruises, scars, poor health, tattered clothing, etc. However, with psychological abuse there are never visible marks. While I count myself lucky that I didn't have to suffer the previously described traumas, I too have unexplained emotional reactions to different stimuli. When these reactions occur, they are usually extremely unpredictable. To an outside observer, this can cause me to appear intolerant or possibly even abusive at times.

Psychological abuse comes in a variety of forms, so it would be inappropriate for me to speculate on all the differences. Some common ones are constant criticism of appearance, negging (manipulating someone using backhanded compliments), gaslighting (manipulating someone into questioning their own perception of reality) and constant threats. In situations involving a narcissist, psychological abuse is commonplace.

During psychological abuse, an abuser will often try to control the victim through fear or belittle them to the point where they give in or give up. In my past, I was often told I was stupid, that I didn't have worth or that I couldn't do anything right. Hearing all this so frequently from people in my life I was supposed to trust the most eventually caused me to believe those statements were true.

I experienced a contradiction to these inputs when I attempted to go to college after high school. Despite having poor grades in high school, I had fantastic grades in my college courses. I didn't understand why, but college was easy for me. *Could it be true that I wasn't stupid?* Nevertheless, I decided to drop out and join the military.

Before joining the United States military, one must take the Armed Services Vocational Aptitude Battery (ASVAB) and score at least 31 to be accepted. I was surprised to discover I scored the maximum of 99. This meant I could intellectually perform any job in the United States Military.

I completed the Army's basic training, then attended Advanced Individual Training (AIT) where I excelled at every stage. After nearly a year, I had learned the equivalent of an associate's degree in electrical engineering. It was a grueling intellectual experience, and I never lost my stride. Though I didn't grasp it at the time, this was proof that what I had been told for so many years about being stupid was completely false. My high ASVAB score and performance under such intellectual rigor was more than enough to dispel those lies.

Psychological abuse is nothing more than lies. It is effective because it often comes from people we trust. The lies are told so often that we become programmed into accepting them as truth. It took me decades to understand I do have value and worth and that I'm not as stupid as I had been told. I was fortunate. Many people subjected to psychological abuse never come to understand the negative things they have been told are lies.

Examine your situation. Do the people in your life consistently drag you down? Do you have to ask permission to leave the house? Are you told you are stupid, worthless, ugly, no good, etc.? Are you told you can't achieve your dreams or that your morals don't matter? Do others threaten you, your loved ones or your pets? Does your partner cheat on you then blame you for it? Do people lie to you regularly? If you answered yes to several of these questions, it is very possible you are in a psychologically abusive environment or relationship.

You *do* have worth.

You are smarter than you realize.

You are valuable.

You are lovable.

You can achieve anything you set your mind to.

Bullying and Discrimination

More than 20% of our society experiences bullying.[11] 91% of Americans experience discrimination in the workplace.[12] Are bullying and discrimination really different?

A bully seeks to harm, intimidate or coerce others, especially if they are perceived as vulnerable.

Someone who discriminates makes an unjust or prejudicial

---

11 www.pacer.org/bullying/info/stats.asp

12 www.cnbc.com/2023/07/27/9percent-of-workers-havent-faced-discrimination-expert-on-what-to-do.html

     Success Unleashed: Mastering Your Life's Purpose

distinction in the treatment of different categories of people, especially on the grounds of ethnicity, sex, age or disability."

Pacer.org states, *"The reasons for being bullied reported most often by students include physical appearance, race/ethnicity, gender, disability, religion, sexual orientation."*

Based on this finding, bullying can be redefined as discrimination with an intent to harm or intimidate. We often point to bullying as something that happens with minors, typically in school. However, bullying doesn't stop once a person graduates. How often have we heard about forms of bullying in the workplace? This could be in the form of mistreating someone based on how they speak, where they come from, what they look like, their sexual orientation, their gender or even something as simple as a past mistake they made which someone just can't let go of.

When we fail to treat others with respect and dignity, we are guilty of engaging in bullying. What starts as gentle teasing can transform into an ongoing habit of degrading the other person. Sometimes this is unintentional, but it's important to note that most of the time we do not know the backgrounds or home situations of our colleagues. We don't know if they ever suffered bullying during school, if they were a victim of physical, sexual or psychological abuse, or how they might react to such an onslaught.

I met a woman several years ago who works for a department within government generally dominated by men. "Julie" told me a story about one of her old bosses who would constantly berate her for her performance. If Julie had been a poor performer, this could have been somewhat justified. However, the data did not justify his treatment of her. There were men in the department who did not perform to the same level as Julie, and they were always given a pass by the same boss.

After examining the facts, Julie escalated a complaint to the head of the department who ruled that her boss was sexually discriminating against her. She left that department and moved to a different agency where she was not challenged but became unhappy with the job itself. However, this was a better alternative than the job she was well-suited to perform under a discriminatory boss.

Julie's story has a silver lining. Her former boss was transferred to another region of the country, and Julie was offered a large promotion to return to her old department. She is no longer subjected to the abuse with which her old boss had tormented her. She is thriving in a senior position with more responsibility and is generally happier in her job.

Julie did the right thing by reporting this behavior. Although the response was not as quick as she would have hoped (nor the fact that she chose a position she didn't enjoy), the former boss eventually faced the consequences of his decision.

When we are being bullied or discriminated against, it is important to responsibly notify the right people; however, this power can be abused. I have seen many cases where discrimination was unfairly filed when it was actually a performance issue. There are bad actors out there who treat people unfairly for things beyond their control. People can't control where they were born, the color of their skin or their gender. A person is no more or less capable because of these attributes, and they should not be treated any differently because of them.

You do not deserve to be treated unfairly. When people

in authority treat others with disrespect and lack of dignity, they demonstrate their lack of character. Unfortunately, too many people reach positions of power and abuse it at the cost of others. If you find yourself subjected to a situation like this, you have the right to seek fair and equal treatment. You have the responsibility to report the abuses so the bad apples can be removed from your environment.

Generational Abuse

People who experience forms of abuse while growing up are six times more likely to become an abuser themselves.[13] Throughout history, we have seen that when parents beat their children, it is predictable they in turn will also beat their children. The same can be said for sexual abuse, psychological abuse, bullying and even infidelity and criminal behavior.

The only way generational abuse can be interrupted is when one generation realizes that what they experienced *was* abuse and chooses to not transfer that same behavior to their own children.

I recently met a man named "Jim." His father was very physically abusive to him growing up. It was the same pattern Jim's father had experienced during his own childhood. Whenever Jim or his brothers would misbehave, their father would take a strap belt and relentlessly whip his sons. The beatings would continue until he was worn out, and the boys were left bleeding and broken. Jim told me that during gym class at school he would refuse to dress down because of the shame he felt in exposing the cuts and bruises he often accumulated during his father's beatings.

---

13   www.reuters.com/article/idUSTRE6BF4MZ

When Jim and his siblings were old enough to have children of their own, they met to discuss the abuses they had all suffered. They agreed it was terrible discipline which could not be allowed to continue to the next generation. Jim and his wife agreed that whenever their children needed discipline, Jim would leave the house to exercise so that discipline could not occur in states of anger. He does believe that spanking as a form of discipline can be administered correctly but never out of anger and never excessively.

My brother and I both struggled with this kind of upbringing, and it began several generations before us. Our father was physically abused and neglected as a child. His mother considered him a burden and treated him as such. She would also document all the things he did wrong throughout the week while his father was away at work. When his father returned home on the weekends, he would review the list of wrongdoings and beat his son savagely as punishment for "tormenting" his mother. This warped my father's sense of appropriate discipline. While he did not pass on the physical abuse, the effects of psychological abuse remained. We were treated horribly and weren't permitted our own thoughts or dignity.

When we entered adulthood, my brother and I made similar decisions with our parenting styles. We came to this conclusion independently and have raised our children without the psychological abuses previously inflicted on us.

Like Jim, I believe there is a time and place for corporal punishment. I established rules to govern my own behavior while raising my children. I was never allowed to spank them unless they violated one of three rules: blatant disobedience, lying or endangering themselves or others. Before spanking one of my kids, I would have to cool off first, then only give the number of spanks reflective of their age. For example, they would receive seven swats for 7 years of age, and it would never be hard enough to leave a mark.

My children have both grown up to be wonderful young women. I can count on one hand how many times I had to spank either of them. They are both well adapted, intelligent, beautiful and loving. Kids always do things that require correction or discipline, but there are ways to teach them right from wrong without violating their dignity, injuring them or creating an otherwise hostile environment. Because I established these self-governing rules, my kids have turned out to be model citizens and have earned the respect of their peers and teachers alike.

We don't have to continue the legacy of abuse we've suffered in our lives. When we can identify the situations above as lies and unhealthy behaviors, we can break the chain of abuse that may have cursed our families for generations. You can be the one to make that change in your family legacy, and it's never too late to start.

Substance Abuse

With so many instances of abuse throughout our society, without appropriate help the victims of abuse will often turn to substances like drugs and alcohol to cope with the stresses and pain they experience so regularly.

According to the National Institute on Drug Abuse,[14] "People use drugs for many reasons: they want to feel good, stop feeling bad, or perform better in school or at work, or

---

14 www.nida.nih.gov

they are curious because others are doing it and they want to fit in." Alcohol, and eventually more serious drugs, can be seen as a quick and easy escape from the pain the user is experiencing.

Unfortunately, while drugs and alcohol can make many people feel good, they have a significant array of side effects that include things like memory loss, paranoia, depression, hallucinations, psychotic and violent behavior, vomiting, lack of coordination, slurred speech, confusion, increased blood pressure and/or heart rate, sores, muscle cramps, tremors, seizures and even death. The symptoms and side effects will vary by substance, and may have long-term effects even after the user has ceased their use.

Along with side effects and the euphoria that comes with substance abuse, it's important to note that addiction will also impact one's ability to achieve purpose. In fact, substance addiction will usually override better judgment, taking over all aspects of a person's life. In addition to hardcore drugs like heroin and methamphetamine, this could include common substances like caffeine or tobacco.

A close friend of mine battled with substance abuse for four years. After suffering a broken shoulder that needed surgical repair, "Greg" got hooked on pain-killers. Once the pain from the surgery had subsided, he told me he would do anything for the fix that came from the pills. He would continue getting prescriptions until he finally ran out of excuses for his doctor. He later turned to obtaining his meds through illegal means. In his words, "It's not the addition itself that causes the most shame. It's what addicts are willing to do to feed it."

     Success Unleashed: Mastering Your Life's Purpose

Greg would count his pills and even engaged in trading other drugs with street dealers so he could feed his addiction. He hid this from his family, and only a few people were aware of the lengths he was willing to go to maintain his habit. When he finally realized he needed to make a change, he couldn't get over the withdrawals without assistance and had to take methadone to get him through it. Now, six years later, he still gets triggered from time to time and is scared to face the reality that he might have to go through the initial recovery process again.

The National Institute on Drug Abuse lists several things that may cause an individual to become addicted to drugs:

- trouble at home
- mental health problems
- trouble in school, at work or trouble making friends
- hanging around other people who use drugs
- starting drug use when young
- individual biology

Having spent over 25 years in environments of extremely high stress (military, energy companies, industrial facilities, high-value sales), I've noticed a trend. The people most likely to have substance abuse issues are those who fail to take appropriate action to deal with stressful conditions.

The military has taken steps to provide much better care of servicemembers who experience traumatic events such as roadside bombs, close combat and indirect fire (missiles, rockets and mortars), but there will likely always be an attitude among service members that they should not seek help. Those service members who adopt this attitude are significantly more likely to develop an addiction to alcohol or other illicit drugs such as cocaine, prescription painkillers or marijuana.

I've seen similar behavior in non-military environments. Workers in industrial facilities tend to favor both alcohol and marijuana. Many oilfield and energy-sector workers struggle with alcohol and marijuana abuse and in more extreme cases cocaine, painkillers and methamphetamine.

Regardless of industry, it is common to find people turning to substances to dull the pain or ease the stress of their jobs or situations. In the attempt to control their mental or emotional state, users of these substances ironically sacrifice their health and can cause themselves severe problems such as stroke, heart attack, seizures and premature death—not to mention additional mental health issues. These habits will eventually cost them more money through prescriptions and visits to the doctor. The pattern may even contribute to more problems like divorce, job loss and jail time.

I have known many people with substance addictions. I've seen too many lives destroyed by these substances to condone their use. I urge you to consider the alternatives over the next two sections. It may be challenging for you to agree with my conclusions, but you may discover one or both are more beneficial than you realize. I've had to swallow my pride several times in life, but I'm almost always thankful in the end. I encourage you to do the same.

It's very important to understand the types of abuse detailed in this chapter. Abuse is like a wall that prevents you from fully realizing your purpose and potentially from even realizing what brings you happiness and joy. The ability to get out from behind addiction or recover from whatever abuse you may have suffered is critical to obtaining the real benefits taught throughout this book.

Therapy

The field of psychology has carried many stigmas throughout the decades. Medical doctors and other hard scientists criticize psychologists for inaccurate science or lack of scientific rigor. They claim that psychology is more subjective than any other branch of science or medicine and that psychologists and psychiatrists too often over-diagnose conditions so they can prescribe more pharmaceuticals.

There are certainly differences in behavior from person to person, and all too often a treatment that works well for one person may not work for another; but there have been many major advances in the field during the past few decades. The ability to more accurately map brain activity while presenting patients with different stimuli has helped clinical psychologists and neurologists develop a better understanding of how the brain works. As a result, practitioners have been able to develop amazing treatment methods that weren't available only a few years ago.

In his book, *The Body Keeps the Score*, Dr. Bessel Van Der Kolk describes several treatment methods such as antipsychotics and other pharmaceuticals, bilateral stimulation like Eye Movement Desensitization and Reprocessing (EMDR), theater therapy and others. After hearing several of my close friends get amazing results from EMDR therapy, I hired a psychologist who specializes in trauma and abuse. I tried EMDR for myself, but it did not work for me.

This realization does not minimize the effectiveness of EMDR, but it does point to the fact that our brains are not all wired the same. My doctor and I have discovered two different treatment methods which have helped me overcome many behaviors that resulted from not having categorized traumas from my youth. Both my friends were stunned when I told them EMDR was ineffective for me, even though it had helped them so much and in a short period of time. Because I was open and honest with my therapist, we were able to shift our focus to different non-pharmaceutical treatments that have helped immensely.

For many generations, people who sought therapy were considered weak and were told there would not be any real help provided during sessions. My guess is that most of those beliefs stemmed from psychology being so widely misunderstood. People who say those things are often scared of what they might learn about themselves. Many people also hold the belief that if they were to be diagnosed with some kind of mental illness they would be treated differently at work, by their primary care physician, their family, the government and more.

When you remove the chains that hold you to your past, you are free to move into the future. By placing more of a focus on mental wellness, I believe many people can escape the bondage of substances to deal with their pasts and the stresses of the present. This will allow thousands, if not millions, of people to move more easily toward the accomplishment of their goals and dreams. It may even allow you to freely discover your purpose and passions.

Faith

Let me start by saying I was not always a man of faith. Because of the abuses I experienced during my childhood and because of the examples I was shown by people who had gone to various church groups, I had decided God was not real. I spent over 20 years of my life as a strong atheist. I didn't believe in what I considered a fairy tale that made people feel better about themselves. I wasn't a militant atheist though; I just preferred to be left alone.

When religious people of any sort tried to push their beliefs on me, I would fight back. During these debates I would unknowingly weaponize my high intelligence against those who were trying to share their truth with me. I could easily shut down most arguments. Because most believers did not demonstrate their own faith, I didn't find debate challenging and was able to defend my position effectively every time.

Eventually I found myself in a private business that consisted of highly devout Christians. One day, I happened to be standing nearby a group that was openly discussing their faith. One of the men asked me how I felt about the topic. I braced myself for an argument and told them I was an atheist. Then they did something I didn't expect. They respected me for who I was and excused themselves to continue their discussion where it wouldn't cause me to be uncomfortable. It was the first time I had ever felt heard and respected by anyone in the religious community.

A few months later, I attended an annual conference with the same company. I was in college at the time as a pre-med student (I did not complete that program), and I understood much about the human body, particularly what was possible and what was not. As one of the company leaders took the main stage, something strange happened before he spoke. I had no prior knowledge of this man or his situation, and he was not given an introduction, but when they announced his name every hair on my body stood on end. I felt like I had just gotten an electrical shock.

I asked the person next to me who this guy was since I wasn't familiar with the executive team. To the amazement of everyone in the room, this man got very sick the year prior and should have died. No one expected him to be on that stage speaking.

For the next 45 minutes this man told his story. He was advanced in age (I recall him being 66 then). A year prior to his story, he was diagnosed with pneumonia that impacted both lungs, and he was hospitalized as a result. He was also diagnosed with a condition called Acquired Adult Respiratory Deficiency Syndrome (AARDS). Based on his age and both medical conditions, he was given a 5% change of survival.

The man's oldest son was a doctor. He was at his father's bedside throughout the entire ordeal. He had also consulted with the attending doctors. They tried everything, but all the vital stats continued to deteriorate. The doctors medically induced a coma, and for weeks there was no progress. They advised the family to start making final arrangements.

Finally, the family made a decision to do a massive, global prayer request. Because of the family's network and the speaker's business connections, they were able to imme-diately reach over 250,000 people with this request. Within two hours of sending the prayer request, all his vital stats began to improve. Everything that needed to go up went up, and everything that needed to go down went down. Three days later he squeezed his wife's hand as he regained consciousness.

The next 90 days were incredibly challenging for this man. He had experienced significant muscle atrophy and needed physical therapy. The doctors said it would be a miracle if he had more than 25% total lung capacity and that the scarring in his lungs would be significant. However, when they examined him, he had almost no scar tissue in his lungs and had over 50% lung capacity in each lung. The doctors said he would never be able to walk unassisted again, but after 90 days of intense physical therapy he walked on his own. I watched him ascend a flight of stairs, walk unassisted across the stage and speak for 45 minutes.

All the education I had about the human body up to that point indicated what I had just witnessed and heard was not possible. How could vital stats, after weeks of deterioration, turn so suddenly in a positive direction after a prayer request was sent? It could not have been possible if it were not so real.

The interaction with the men speaking their faith in the office helped me be receptive to the experience I just described. The absolute impossibility of the story showed me I might just be wrong in my stance as an atheist. In that moment, before the man left the stage, I knew there was a supreme power in the Universe.

For the next few months, I went on a journey to understand what had just happened. I discovered for myself that Christianity was the only religion that made any sense.

During my search for the truth, I attended countless different religious services. Some were based on what appeared to be nothing more than tradition, while others tended to deal only with feelings and didn't offer any notable foundation. Christianity was built on the foundation of Judaism; but Jesus of Nazareth not only spoke with unprecedented wisdom, He also fulfilled prophecies that were written hundreds or even thousands of years before he was born.

Christianity offered hope for me where no other religious group could. For over 20 years, I have lived as a Christian. The number of miracles I've witnessed first-hand continues to amaze me. The depth of my understanding of the Christian religion has grown deeper, and it's even more fascinating today than it was in my initial exploration of my faith.

If you have not explored the possibility that there is a God or that Jesus of Nazareth did walk the Earth performing miracles only to be crucified by the Romans, let me encourage you to research it for yourself. Regarding abuse, I've seen miracles where people overcame addiction, mended broken relationships and healed from terrible diseases. I have personally been to the point of considering suicide and have struggled with depression only to be pulled out and blessed beyond anything I could have dreamed.

You might struggle with this idea, and that's okay. The idea of an invisible deity who could speak the world into existence was impossible for me to believe. But if you open your mind to the possibility and seek to find Him (rather than disprove Him), there is evidence of creation everywhere you look.

For example, if we don't consider God as the creator of the

Universe, why do Venus, Uranus and only one of the moons of Neptune spin in a different direction than all the other planets in our solar system? If the Big Bang is true, why don't those planets and moons follow the Law of Conservation of Angular Momentum?

Therapy and faith are simply two alternatives that can help abuse survivors to reconcile their pasts. Many other outlets are available such as Alcoholics Anonymous, Narcotics Anonymous, Celebrate Recovery, Advocate Safehouses, Domestic Shelters, and online resources such as the National Domestic Violence Hotline, Hope Recovery, Fort Refuge, Love Is Respect, and Male Survivor. Many more resources can be found within your local community based on the type of abuse you may be recovering from.

What's the point of all this?

Regardless of the abuse you may have suffered or are suffering, it is critical in your journey of discovering your purpose and achieving of your goals that you find a way to untie the knots applied to your life. If you haven't been the victim of abuse, please be considerate of others; it can be incredibly difficult to fully understand the people around us and the burdens they carry. As you work with a therapist or with a member of the clergy, understand it may take time to get to the point where you can move forward. There is a process involved, and you will become even more amazing than you are today as you go through it. Enjoy the journey, and trust the process.

You are worth the effort. You are worthy of the investment to achieve your purpose, passion and dreams.

I can't wait to see the man or woman you become!

Chapter 3
Society and the RUT

"Peer pressure and social norms are powerful influ-
ences on behavior, and they are classic excuses."

—Andrew Lansley on Obesity

One of the strongest forces in any society is peer pressure. Our society tells us what to wear, how to behave, who we should date and even where we should live. Anyone who deviates from those societal norms is labeled an outcast and largely rejected by society. This applies not only to the nation or the state in which we live, but can go all the way down to the family level.

If our parents or spouses expect us to behave in a particular way, it can cause division if we deviate. I've seen many instances where someone remains in a job they hate simply because it is what they are expected to do.

One client of mine is a perfect example of this expectation. After college, "Eddie" joined the US military, serving as an officer for several years. Because of the nature of his job and the expected benefits that continuing service to the Federal government provided, he chose to work for the government when he left military service. At the time of his military separation, jobs were scarce; most of the companies he tried to work for chose not to hire him.

Eddie found himself in a department run by a leader unwilling to do what was right for the team. As a result, Eddie's job caused him many medical issues due to the stress he was constantly under. Fortunately, he was able to shift under different leadership after a few years. His new leader invested in him, enabling him to earn certifications he will need to further his career.

I had dinner with Eddie after working with him for several years. He confided in me that despite the new and significantly better leadership, he is still under tremendous stress because of his job. His department strongly favors doctorate-level college degrees, and because his highest education level is a masters, his earning potential is severely limited.

I asked him why he doesn't shift to the private sector where potential is much higher. He said it was because he is working toward his pension, and his government medical benefits are too good to walk away from. He's also afraid the tempo of a private sector job would overwhelm him. He feels he would not be able to assimilate to a job where he could thrive outside the government.

Eddie's family also has a history of government service. Many of them have retired and are continuing to reap the pension benefits they worked so hard to earn. This adds additional pressure to Eddie whenever he considers shifting his career strategy toward anything other than his current occupation.

The world in which Eddie works is all he knows. He is one of the most intelligent people I've had the pleasure of working with. The norms of his community dictate he should continue working for the government, and there is perceived pressure placed on him due to his family history. He feels helpless to make a career move that could increase his earning potential which could better support his family.

Does this mean Eddie has made a bad decision by choosing this career field? Absolutely not. He continues to receive outstanding reviews every year, and his new leadership regularly recognizes him for his contributions. Each year at his facility is another year closer to his pension. The government also provides much-needed medical benefits for his family. His commitment and attention to detail make him extraordinary at what he does, and his efforts help his department function more efficiently.

Like many of you who are reading this book, Eddie feels that the pressure of moving away from the known and into the unknown can feel insurmountable. Changing jobs, let alone career fields, is a radically stressful event. When finances are lean or health concerns must be considered, it can sometimes feel much better to do nothing rather than make a change.

When I finished high school, I tried to follow the social convention of my peers by going to college right away. This ended miserably for me. At the time, I just wasn't ready. Before I get into that, I'll back up a few years and explain more about where I was coming from.

Very few people have stories about thriving their entire lives, and my story is no different. Earlier I described some of the abuse I struggled with in my family and in school. There was also an internal struggle I wasn't aware of. Being isolated and socially awkward was a horrible combination for me because of how I'm wired.

According to the Myers Briggs Type Indicator (MBTI) personality test, I am an ESTP.[15] This means I'm Extroverted (gathers energy from other people versus Introverted which gets drained by them), Sensory (uses senses to collect information about the environment versus Intuition which applies gut feelings), Thinking (favors logic over emotion when making decisions versus Feeling which favors emotions over logic), and Perceiving (prefers flexibility and spontaneity versus Judging which favors structure and order).

I'm extroverted by nature. Being so isolated and awkward meant I internally felt like my environment and everyone in it was against me. I was in a constant state of depression. I turned to food for comfort (a problem I still struggle with) and couldn't see any good in the world around me. By the time I graduated high school, I had found a few friends, but I had not yet found my rhythm in social circles. This meant I had not yet gotten to a point of solid social or psychological recovery.

My emotional wounds were still fresh when I tried going to college, so I couldn't deal with the stresses of that environment. I did well in math and science because they were suitable to my logical nature. I was trying to balance being a student with a job and trying to understand who I was. My emotions were about as stable as a two-legged chair.

I watched my high school peers thriving in college, but

---

15 eu.themyersbriggs.com/en/tools/MBTI/MBTI-personality-Types

I wasn't ready for the challenge. I was fortunate enough to find my first mentor while in a health and fitness class. I don't remember anything specific he said or did that created such a lasting impact, but Professor Arnold drew something out of me I never understood was there. He helped me find the social side of myself and to become more comfortable with who I was deep down. It would take me many more years to fully grasp that, but I have pinpointed this change in my life to my experience in Professor Arnold's class. *Thank you, Mike!*

I eventually dropped out of college because of my inability to manage the stresses of balancing that with work and what little social life I had. I knew I still needed to get an education, but the timing wasn't right for me. I needed to develop emotionally and continue discovering myself before I could embark on a formal education. If I had continued to follow the social pressure all around me, I may have ended up in a worse place than where my life-choices took me.

I need to point out that not all social pressure is bad. Amid the negative social media, cyber-bullying and disinformation, there are positives about the world being so interconnected. Without social pressure our society would not have gotten to the point where we are today.

People have become much more aware of bad health choices such as cigarettes. We're more aware of the social injustice of racism and sexism. Social media has helped us to demand and receive better service from professionals throughout our communities. As we continue to evolve as a society, I remain hopeful that the negatives of social media will eventually be snuffed out so the positives can rise to the top. It could be a driving force for growth throughout our culture.

Why do you do what you do? Is it because you earn a lot of money yet are otherwise miserable? Is it because you feel expected to do it by your family or society? Is it because you felt you were too far along a path to make a change? Is it because you're afraid to pursue your passion? Maybe it's because you haven't found your passion.

Perhaps you know what you are passionate about. Maybe your job meets your life's purpose, but you haven't been able to gain the traction you need to move forward. Maybe you haven't yet gained the skills or experience necessary to fully thrive. There might be others in your work environment who are creating extra work, chaos or obstacles which you constantly fight. Maybe you need to overcome a mess someone before you had left behind.

Sometimes the RUT we find ourselves in has little or nothing to do with our own purpose or passion but is impacted by external circumstances. This is understandably a very challenging scenario, and there are several alternatives to be considered. While your goals are still worthy of being developed and vetted, it may also be worthwhile to have others around you develop their goals. Determine if they belong, but proceed with caution; you don't want to appear like you're trying to get them to leave.

Maybe you are in the right position but in the wrong company or department. If you know you're doing the right task, it may be worth discussing with your leadership what other alternatives there are for you within your organization. There are likely dozens of other alternatives to consider depending on your unique circumstances.

If you are one of the more fortunate people in a job or

course of study that excites you, congratulations! When you are able to do what you truly love, your work doesn't feel like a chore. However, even if you love what you do, it's still important for you to understand your purpose and develop goals. You have simply conquered a major stumbling block many of your contemporaries encounter.

When we are not following our purpose or don't feel success while pursuing it, our jobs can feel horrible. It can be difficult or even impossible to find fulfillment. We can be overwhelmed by stress or depression. We may jump from job to job trying to advance our career or shift into a different function so we can find *it* (whatever *it* is). When this happens, we find ourselves in a RUT—Rude, Ugly and Tired. (It's a terrible acronym, but some of you will remember it.)

When we're in a RUT we lose the hope that we can make a change in the world. We become bitter, which often tends to manifest around our loved ones. This can result in damaged or lost friendships and marriages. Our reputations can suffer, and finding new jobs can become even more difficult because of that.

Okay, JP... This is all great, but how am I supposed to figure out what my purpose is?

You are not alone in asking this question. Most adults I've met will admit they still don't know what they want to do when they grow up.

I mentioned earlier that most people do what works or what is expected of them. All too often it's because they haven't discovered their purpose or passion; or if they have discovered it, they don't know how to make a career out of it.

When you can uncover how to make a career out of your purpose, you will be so amazing at it that the money will eventually follow.

If someone had told me earlier in life that I would be a life coach and professional speaker, I would have called them crazy. I didn't understand that helping other people level-up their lives would be the most exciting thing in the world to me. I didn't expect getting on stage with a microphone would be the most effective way for me to accomplish my life's purpose. It took me years of doing things I hated before I finally found my purpose. Regardless of the time it takes, you will find your purpose if you dig in and do the work outlined in this book.

In chapter seven I briefly discuss WISE goal setting. This is designed for you to better understand the underlying reason behind each of your personal and professional goals. The same root cause analysis we use in the WISE system can be used to help you find your passions.

We leverage the 5 Whys technique (invented in the 1930s by Japanese industrialist Sakichi Toyoda) to identify what is ultimately driving your goals. In using this technique I discovered that one of my goals was not actually my goal. WISE goal setting has helped me shift my strategies and redefine my goals to be more in alignment with where I need to be for ultimate fulfillment.

When we use this for discovering our purpose, we can examine the things that make us feel happy, fulfilled and excited. We can ultimately get to the point where we find true purpose and passion.

My daughter is incredibly intelligent but has no idea what she wants to do with her life. During our day-to-day conversations, I've discovered she has a genuine interest in how the human body works. She is also excellent at math and science, but she doesn't want to pursue those because science is "icky" (she doesn't want to do dissections).

She struggles in several social areas, so being a doctor might not be the best option for her. However, if she were to work as a scientist, it could give her the opportunity to study how chemicals function within the human body without necessarily having to work directly with patients. Her ability to ask challenging questions is far beyond her education level, and she does it frequently. I'm convinced she was *born* for the fields of biology, physiology or chemistry.

She will need to discover her own path. I will guide her to discover her purpose, but ultimately that realization is hers. Once she discovers the root of her natural curiosity, she will have the ability to find true happiness and fulfillment because she'll be able to do what she was meant to do. I will be there for her when she is ready to do the work of the 5 Whys.

Finding a good coach or mentor familiar with root cause analysis can help you dig in and find the underlying things that cause you to be happy. It's best to give them a list of things that make you happy or excite you so you'll have something to work with. The chart below is based on the 5 Whys technique. I strongly recommend using a coach or mentor to guide you through this. Trying to do the exercise on your own can lead to unintended biases which will give you false results.

 Success Unleashed: Mastering Your Life's Purpose

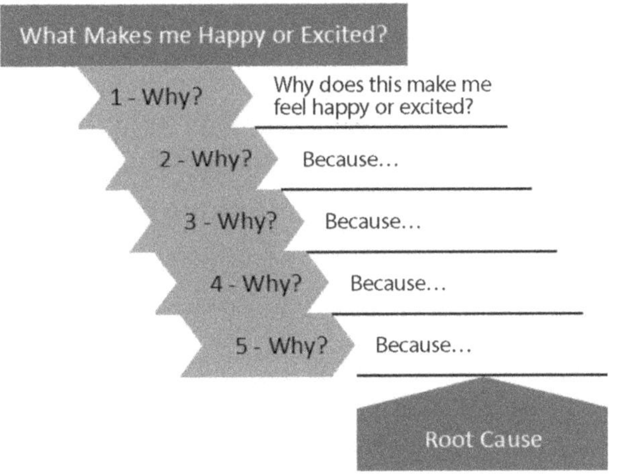

Don't worry if it takes several attempts to figure out what your purpose actually is. Certain things may be clouding your judgment which can make it difficult for you to answer some of the questions. You may also find it difficult to go beyond a certain point while using this technique. A few reasons might be

- incorrect or inaccurate answers during previous steps;
- clouded judgment due to external circumstances such as abuse, trauma, poor relationships or other psychological issues; or
- poorly worded "why" questions.

You may also discover you don't need all 5 Whys or that 5 aren't enough. You and your coach should be able to make that determination. However, I do want to emphasize the need to trust this process. Finding your purpose may be more fun than understanding the root cause of your goals, but as you begin to get deeper this will still feel like work. That's okay. The more effort you put into understanding this part of yourself, the more you are going to discover why certain things make you happy or excited.

The biggest benefit to this is that you can be much more intentional in all your activities whether for work or pleasure. You may also realize that your purpose and what you are passionate about lead to different hobbies. From here, your life will be more fulfilling and your stress levels are very likely to decrease by pursuing your true purpose.

Once you've uncovered your purpose you will have a new super power! You can make decisions for yourself, and they won't be based on what is best according to peers, friends or family. Your education can be guided by what fuels your passions the most. Your career choices will be guided by *your* internal compass, not by what someone else wants for you. You will have a much higher likelihood of becoming successful. Maybe you will switch majors, change companies, switch job functions or move to a different part of the country or world.

If you haven't yet found Mr. or Mrs. Right, perhaps the root cause exercise can help you narrow down the traits you need in your future spouse. Knowing yourself better will give you the power to take control of your life in a way you've never had. It will allow you to use the BIAS method more effectively as you work through this book.

Chapter 4
Relationships

"Networking is not about just connecting people. It's about connecting people with people, people with ideas and people with opportunities."

—Michele Jennae

You may have heard that *Your Network is Your Net Worth*, which is also a book by Porter Gale; but do you really understand what this means? For years, I had heard this statement but couldn't wrap my head around what it could possibly mean. Growing up in the conditions I did and with a sour taste for leadership, I was never shown the benefit of having a strong personal network. Consequently, I couldn't see the value of having a strong network of people in my life.

I have come to understand that leadership is not a negative force but an incredibly powerful one. I have begun to understand the people we surround ourselves with can help us get into new jobs and positions. They can also shape our minds, open us to new experiences and opportunities, and help us grow our value throughout our communities. Ironically, networking is not about what you can get but ultimately what you can give. By giving more of ourselves and sharing what we know to help others grow, we will find ourselves learning and growing in the process.

It's important to highlight that getting started might not feel comfortable to you. Feeling anxious about doing something you've never done before is a completely normal response. Even after networking for years, I still feel some discomfort about stepping into a new environment for the first time. *What do they do here? What do they expect me to do? What does "normal" behavior look like? Who are the right people to engage with?* These are all common feelings and questions. The most important thing is that you take the first step. It's likely people will offer their hands to introduce themselves, and that's all you will need to take the first step.

Another consideration is how comfortable you are with people. Depending on which study you read, introverts make up 25-40% of the population, so it's possible you fall into that category. Maybe you don't like small talk, or it's stressful to have a discussion with a stranger. It can also feel exhausting to be around people for too long. This is all okay.

Do some research before you go to a networking event and be sure to note how long the event is scheduled to last. You should also ask about protocols when you arrive in case you feel the need to leave early. However, don't use this as an excuse to limit yourself or to procrastinate in getting started. Every day you fail to take this first step is another day you delay reaching your full potential.

Building a social network and a professional network

are not necessarily the same thing. We need people in our lives who can help us relax and who we genuinely enjoy being around. Our friends are an important part of our lives because they are the people in whom we can confide, and they can help us unwind from the busy lives we live. However, friends may not be the ones who can help us grow the most. They may not be the ones you will likely rely on to help build your professional value. Of course, there are some who may fall into both your social and professional networks; but these are exceptions, not the rule.

A professional network needs to be built intentionally. There are a few necessary questions that should be explored as you begin this process so you can efficiently embark on this part of your journey.

- In which areas of life are you trying to improve?
- Who do you already know with the skills you need? Are they willing to mentor you? Can they introduce you to their network so you can learn from their mentors?
- Who have you worked with in the past with whom you have a good relationship? They may be able to make key introductions to you, either for a new job or position or to their extended networks.
- What is your availability? Being intentional about building your network means you may have to give up some things that aren't feeding you. The TV won't miss you. Video games can't help you. What can you cut out of your life to have a brighter future? What days and times can you free up on a regular basis to enhance your future?

- What do you have to offer? A major part of building your network is not about what you can get from the interaction but what you can give along the way. If you have an expectation of getting something, you will never achieve the results you want. However, if you engage in networking with the intent of providing something to others, you will ultimately grow more than you could ever imagine.
- Knowing the areas where you have something to offer allows you to enter into relationships with a mindset of generosity, and the benefits will soon follow. Trust this process. It works, but you must give it time.
- What groups, lodges, societies, clubs, etc. are available in your area? Once you've gone through your immediate network, you'll need to venture out on your own to find people you don't already know.

Speaking of clubs, I've had tremendous success building my network through Toastmasters International, a global non-profit organization that teaches speaking and leadership skills. Consider Rotary International, a global non-profit organization committed to providing service, promoting integrity and advancing world understanding, goodwill and peace. There are hundreds of groups like these, so feel free to research and explore what might be best for you.

Once you've begun your networking process, you will need to identify the types of relationships you want and need. I encourage you to explore them as much as your resources will allow. Keep in mind that at different points throughout

    Success Unleashed: Mastering Your Life's Purpose

your networking journey, the nature of these relationships may necessarily have to change. Allow those changes to occur, because you will always be growing. Unless you are willing to allow your network to expand, you may be limiting your own potential.

There is some debate about the difference between mentors and coaches. My definitions are based on my own experiences and gleaned through my training and certifications. It is important you know the types of relationships you need in your network and that you use each one as necessary according to its type.

Mentors

When you learn something new, whether a skill, task, job or mindset, you won't necessarily possess the background or training necessary to move forward without assistance. In a work environment you will likely receive training that will give you the basics, but they rarely provide you with the tribal knowledge or muscle memory necessary for being ultimately successful. Some of this comes from repetition of daily tasks, but it can be accelerated by the hiring of a mentor.

Mentors are experts in a particular area who can provide you with the information necessary to be more efficient and effective. They will tell you what to do or how to do something. A great boss will function both as a mentor and as a coach and glide gracefully between the two as your skillset develops. Colleagues or supervisors may also fill the mentor role for you.

It is extremely important for you to be open-minded when working with a mentor. They give you their time and knowledge, so don't take this for granted. If you fail to respect these relationships, they can quickly dissolve; and you could be stuck in a situation where you are not able to grow at the rate you need to thrive.

A mentoring relationship is not always a one-way street. As with your professional network, it will serve you when working with one if you are able to offer something in return. Try to find ways you can add value to the relationship or consider finding areas where you are capable of mentoring them. This can transform a mentoring relationship into a symbiotic relationship.

Coaches

Once you've developed a baseline of skills or try to do something that hasn't been done before, you will sometimes find yourself at the end of your creativity. This is where coaches come into play. In comparison, athletic coaches don't necessarily have the same skills or ability as the players, but they know how to draw out the best in each of them. The same can be said for professional life or business coaches. You have a unique set of skills and abilities. Perhaps you have excelled in your career to get you to where you are today. A coach will ask questions that draw out the best answer by leveraging your creativity.

This is different from mentors who already know their craft and give you the answers. Coaches will not often have the answer, but they do understand how to ask powerful questions.

Like mentors, coaches should always be regarded with a level of trust. They don't necessarily know the specifics of

   Success Unleashed: Mastering Your Life's Purpose

your job, but when you build trust with your coach, the benefits can be huge. Take the time to allow your coach-client relationship to develop trust by being open. Coaching is only effective when both people trust one another.

Finally, coaching relationships must be handled with confidentiality. If your coach is within your company, he or she may eventually leave. You may sometimes share information intended for internal use only. While trust is a fundamental element, it is also prudent to take necessary precautions. Even the most well-intentioned people can make judgment errors from time to time. If you hire an external coach, be sure to have some kind of non-disclosure agreement (NDA) in place to protect the interests of your company and to hold your coach legally responsible if sensitive information ever gets disclosed.

Symbiotic

I find symbiotic relationships most fulfilling. If you can enter a relationship with the attitude of giving, you open the other person's ability to give back to you. You may occasionally develop relationships with others that allow you to grow from each other.

I have a wonderful friend with whom I've been working for over five years. She and I call each other frequently to work through challenges each of us may face. We are both certified coaches, so this allows us to ask the right questions to find solutions to our problems. We also have the level of trust which allows us to verbally smack one another in the head when something doesn't feel right.

Symbiotic relationships can turn into deep friendships. They allow us to bond through mutual vulnerability and growth. They don't always need to be coach- or mentor-based; but when those principles are applied, they allow both parties in the relationship to continuously grow and shape one another.

Peers

Similar to symbiotic relationships, peers can be critically important. Don't confuse peers with friends, though. Friends are the people you enjoy being around, but they are not always the ones who can push you. Peers, on the other hand, may be colleagues, neighbors or competitors you are close to with whom you share similar responsibilities.

In my sales career there was a person who was both a colleague and my internal competition. Within the sales world progress is often measured in years, halves, quarters or months. In our case, it was quarters. For 16 quarters, my colleague and I competed to see who would have better sales numbers, and I lost an incredible 14 of those quarters. I was so frustrated, but I learned a lot from him. I never made it easy for him to win, and we were often within two or three percent of one another.

His competitive nature wouldn't allow him to lose, and my ability to earn customers' trust kept the sales rolling in, so we grew together. As the team expanded, we collectively pushed one another. One year, all six of us team members earned the highest award given by the company. Our sales engineers and our leadership also won top honors. In all, 10 people earned the President's Club award and a company vacation because we refused to stop competing.

 Success Unleashed: Mastering Your Life's Purpose

Not all jobs are sales, of course. When we can take the time to learn from our peers, grow from them and share failures with them, everyone is better as a result.

This is also not limited to our careers. I play drums as a hobby. I will never command the stage like some iconic drummers who have made millions of dollars in their career; but my technique, timing, speed and the arrangement of my drum set have all developed from observing my peers. YouTube knows I love to watch drumming videos, and although the drummers in those videos will not likely ever meet me, they are still my peers.

Our peers can push us in ways many others cannot because they are in similar situations as we are. They know what we are going through, and we can celebrate and commiserate with them equally.

Pro-bono

Regardless of how the relationship is built, there will always be a difference between paid and volunteered. *Pro-bono* relationships happen when one person genuinely wants to help another. These are great for the recipient and can help get a person started, especially if they are new in a career field or an area in which they are trying to grow.

Many of the mentors and coaches I've had throughout my life have come from the volunteer organizations I've been a part of. Through it all, it is important not to misuse or abuse those people who give freely of their time and skills to help you grow.

In his book, *How to Win Friends and Influence People,* Dale Carnegie says to "be hearty in your approbation and lavish in your praise." When someone is willing to give of themselves for the betterment of others, the biggest gift you can give them in return is your heartfelt appreciation. Some people have difficulty in expressing their gratitude because they aren't sure how it's going to be received.

If that describes you, please consider giving praise anyway if someone has done something for you. If they choose to receive it as anything other than gratitude, that's on them. In my experience, most people do not react negatively to gratitude. In fact, many people crave it because it has become so rare in our society. When you give praise and gratitude for being helped through your struggles, this gives them the fuel they need to continue doing that for you and for others.

Professional

Mentors and coaches receive payment for the services they provide. You are much more likely to find professional coaches than mentors; but like great bosses, great coaches (especially those who have specific areas of expertise) may also glide smoothly between coaching and mentoring.

Within this category you are much more likely to find people who hold certain certifications such as a life or career coach, among many others. Many of these professionals are more knowledgeable in specific areas, so it's a good idea to take time to research a coach before you sign a contract. If you have a specific goal in mind, it may not be the best use of your resources to work with a coach who specializes in a totally different area.

These professionals won't usually have detailed information about your job and may not even have worked in that sector, so you may need to interpret how you see that in the relationship. Since you'll be entering into a contract and spending hard-earned money for the guidance they provide, you must do your homework and get everything you're after from the business relationship.

Professionals also differ from *pro-bono* mentors and coaches by the duration of the relationship. They seek stability in their businesses, so they are likely to continue staying with you as long as you are willing to continue paying them. Those who volunteer their time do not have the same level of interest in the relationship and may not be as consistent or predictable as those you pay. Because of this, professionals are much more likely to gain a deeper understanding of you and your needs over time. You stand to gain quite a bit more from these engagements.

There is one key highlight about all these relationships. In these circumstances, the people with whom you align are working to build you up. They do not *do* your work for you. Ultimately, you are the one who is responsible to take action on the knowledge you receive from your coaches, mentors, etc. They are there to help you grow, but you've got to do the work along the way. They can point you in the right direction, but it's impossible to steer a parked car.

In the previous segment you read about giving praise and respect to those you draw into your network. Another critical element in developing your network is your reputation. As you move between organizations, mentors and coaches, many people you encounter will have networks of their own.

If you develop a reputation as someone who always takes and never gives back, or if you disrespect those who try to help, you are likely to discover fewer people willing to help you. Eventually, those who are willing to help you in the beginning will figure it out and move on. Take my advice and don't let that person be you. Your reputation matters.

Now that you've got the basics about how to take the first steps in building your network, where do you go from here?

It is critical you start this process intentionally. When you begin your networking journey, you will encounter many different people. If you are not clear about what you hope to give and receive in the process, it can be very overwhelming.

As you begin to meet people, you will know intuitively if they are able to help you reach your goals. Often, they will not be the right people for you, and that's okay; but that doesn't mean you should write them off. Instead, let them know what you intend to bring to a networking relationship and how you are trying to grow. They may be able to make an introduction to another person who can bring you to where you want to be.

Remember to help people with something in return. This will not only help you reach your goals faster, but it will bolster your reputation along the way. You never know if you will have a need down the road for a person who can't help you in the moment.

The more you attend networking events and interact with people, the more opportunities you will have to develop relationships that will help you grow. This will become more natural as you do it, so getting started is truly the most important step in the entire process.

Developing your network can be fun. You will meet new and interesting people. You will have opportunities for new experiences and may even discover new interests along the way. When this happens it can be extremely tempting to dive in more than you had originally intended.

On the other side of the coin, I cannot overstate the need for balance in your life, especially If you are married or otherwise have a family that depends on you. Yes, it is crucial to get up from the couch to develop your network; but it's equally important to continue building the network within your family. Your spouse should be your single biggest supporter, so you should be there for them as well. Your children (if you have them) also need you, both as a role model and for emotional support.

I am very passionate. When I find a new area of interest, I dive in head first and completely absorb myself in my new adventure. I am an extreme extrovert, so being around people is akin to being hooked on a drug. This has been great for the development of my network, learning new skills and helping others to build theirs. However, you should be aware that imbalance in your life is a nasty side-effect.

Don't ignore your family or friends. While you should invest in yourself and build your network, it is equally important to invest in those closest to you. Mistakes will be made from time to time, but they will be there to pick you up during the hard times. I've made mistakes with my family from time to time, and I've also made up for them every chance I get. They know they will always be my first priority no matter how excited I get during my adventures. If you fail to take care of your family, you are ultimately failing yourself.

Chapter 5
Realization and Decision

*"With the realization of one's own potential
and self-confidence in one's ability,
one can build a better world."*

—Dalai Lama

For much of my life I was fed information I believed to be true. Maybe you can relate to that statement.

My parents did a fantastic job at demonstrating an incredibly good work ethic while I was growing up. Despite both being retired, they are still some of the hardest working people I know. They keep themselves occupied, and they have always approached everything with an extreme degree of excellence. They worked efficiently and diligently to make sure everything was done right. They devoted themselves to every assigned task. I have always applied their same tenacity and willingness to complete my own projects.

There were several downsides, however. My dad worked as a construction laborer for most of his professional life before he opened his own interior carpentry business. He was great at what he did and loved it very much. When he moved the family across the country in the early 1980s, he embarked on designing and building his own house.

He was not its general contractor, nor did he hire a construction company to build what he designed. He did almost all the work by himself. He dug the foundation by hand, ran septic lines, framed the house, ran the wiring, ran the well into the house and installed the windows and doors. He even did the roof with minimal help.

The rest of the family was enlisted to help where we could. I was too young to help with the big projects, but I did help quite a bit with the painting, sanding and some of the digging. I even bellied through the crawl space with a flashlight to help him run wiring.

Throughout this process, my dad enforced his own standards of work. We rarely took breaks. Lunches were very short (I learned to eat fast) and we never stopped working until the job for that day was finished. Sometimes that would be late into the night after a very early start in the morning.

When I was old enough to have my first "real" job away from the family, I was surprised I was required to take regular breaks. If someone worked more than six hours in a shift, they were mandated two 15-minute breaks and a 30-minute lunch. I didn't understand why I needed a break in the first place. I didn't know what to do with all that time. After working with my dad for so many years, a six- or eight-hour shift felt like I was just starting my day.

My peers didn't like how I was outperforming them, and management didn't appreciate me not wanting to take breaks. I had to learn to comply with labor laws and people who didn't grow up under my same conditions. I learn very quickly and have achieved the highest ratings in nearly every job I've had. Part of my maturation process was learning how to be tactful, so I eventually got to the point where I could succeed without evoking resentment from my peers.

I mentioned earlier how the abuse during my parents' upbringing created a mental construct that was reinforced upon entering their adult lives. The authority figures and leadership they were exposed to early in their careers contributed to a very poor outlook on leaders.

When my parents (more often my dad) came home from work, I would regularly hear about how terrible their bosses were. They described them using creative and fully abusive terms. I heard how they were good-for-nothing and how they sat in their ivory towers barking out orders on how to do tasks they didn't know how to do.

Leaders were presented to me as horrible people who treated subordinates terribly. They made too much money for what little they did, and they only served to make life more difficult for everyone around them. Because of their mentality toward leadership, neither of my parents sought that out; and it wouldn't likely have been offered to them anyway.

I did not fully understand my parents' childhood and their subsequent attitude toward leadership, but I unknowingly adopted that same attitude. Their strong work ethic served me well as I entered the workforce, but my misunderstanding of leadership held me back considerably throughout my early career.

I joined the working world as soon as I was able and applied the same work ethic instilled in me. After a few entry jobs in food service and retail, I decided it was time for me to pursue a long-term and stable career path. In the Army, I had no expectation the leadership would be any better than what was described to me in the past. As I reflect on my life, though, I now realize good leadership was always around me. I just didn't recognize it at the time for what it was. Several bad leaders did reinforce the opinion I had grown up with.

Although the drill sergeants were tough as nails, they were actually fantastic leaders. However, after training, I wound up in a unit with one of the worst platoon sergeants. He was one of the most selfish, egocentric and unrealistically demanding people I've ever met. He did not have his soldiers' best interests in mind, and he almost never recognized the hard work of those who reported to him. This did nothing but reinforce my negative perception of leadership.

After leaving the Army, it was more of the same for me—bad boss after bad boss. I encountered leaders who would neglect their people and treat them so poorly that they left as quickly as they could. Because of these bad bosses I developed a pattern of leaving jobs after one year. My wife knew that every March I would begin working for a different company.

This pattern continued for about five years until I finally found a job where I didn't have to see my boss every day. The independence I felt in that stage of my career allowed me to remain for two, then three years.

Because of my parents' low opinion of leadership, I never

wanted such a position in my career; but as I got older, leadership began to look more appealing. Army life and other manual jobs were physically demanding over the years, and the physical toll on my body was becoming evident. My knees hurt constantly, and I discovered I had torn my ACL and both meniscuses nearly ten years prior. My back was in so much pain that I would eat six Advil and six Aleve every day just so I could stand. Something had to change, or I would likely end up in a wheelchair or require major surgery.

Earlier, I mentioned a college professor who had demonstrated wonderful leadership. I also tried to work with a multi-level marketing company whose top priority was the development of leaders. The leaders in that organization were all about personal growth books. They had a mantra which always stuck with me: "Leaders are readers." I took that to heart. Those leaders were so passionate about leadership that I couldn't help but believe them despite my misgivings.

I have read hundreds of personal development and leadership books; but regardless of how many books I read, I never felt I applied what I learned. I had only seen a few examples of good leadership, so it wasn't nearly enough to reinforce what the authors were telling me.

In 2016, I was a field electrician for an oilfield company. In prior years I had made my living working with electrical automation and was extremely good at my craft. If you owned any stock in 2016, you may remember it was a terrible year for the energy sector. It was also a terrible year to be employed by an energy company. I got laid off. By the time I entered the job market, there were zero jobs where my skills could amount to anything. For six weeks my full-time occupation was looking for a job, and I was striking out everywhere. Eventually, a friend of mine who worked at a major computer company offered me a job in software renewals.

I had no interest or experience with computers other than using them to create documents or send emails. I didn't know what software was or why it would need to be renewed. Though I had dabbled in sales early in my career, I had never been successful with it and had no interest in becoming a career salesperson. Also, this job offered only 17% of my previous income. Regardless, I accepted the offer because it allowed me to go broke a little slower. It wasn't the job I was hoping for, but it was offered to me through the network I had developed. My friend knew me well enough to offer me the position. This life transition eventually paid off for me.

You may be wondering what this has to do with a success mindset or the discovery of your purpose. When you find yourself in a RUT, there is a point when you realize something in your life needs to change. I had been working successfully as a robotics engineer and avoiding leadership because I didn't want to end up like one of the "evil" people I heard my parents describe.

The books I read helped to reshape the belief that not all leaders are horrible, but I still had not experienced much good leadership in my own career. This all changed with the loss of my career and the shift to IT sales.

When I started my new position, I found myself in a completely unfamiliar environment. I was surrounded by people who knew more than I did about everything in this arena. Suddenly, all the personal development books I had been reading for the past couple of decades began to make sense. Several recurring themes now made sense and needed to be applied if I was going to survive in the corporate jungle.

The first and perhaps biggest lesson I had learned through all the books was to find a mentor. I became obsessed with learning this new industry and developing the techniques that had helped others become successful in their careers. I also talked with every manager and director in the facility. Imagine my surprise when I discovered the leaders were regular people who wanted those under them to succeed.

This was a huge revelation for me. Up to this point, leaders were nothing to be admired and didn't do or want anything good for their subordinates. I had finally discovered an environment where its leaders mirrored those portrayed in all my books.

If you are stuck in your career, you may possibly have a misguided belief. My parents didn't mean to steer me wrong about leadership; they were simply relaying their experiences. To a young and impressionable mind, though, it created a belief that all leaders were like those they experienced. Consider these questions to help determine if there are falsehoods in your life or career:

- When you read, do you consistently find scenarios that do not align with your experience?
- Do you see other people seemingly less equipped than yourself reaching the level of success you want?
- Do you wake up every day dreading your job or your boss?
- Will your current job or position help you to get where you want or need to be in your career?

 Success Unleashed: Mastering Your Life's Purpose

There are many other books out there that can help you. For example, *From Good to Great* (Jim Collins) is business oriented but can also be applied to personal journeys. *Who Moved my Cheese?* (Spencer Johnson) is a quick read and anecdotal about being willing to change our mindsets. I highly recommend anything by John Maxwell for leadership and success. You might want to start with *Success is a Choice*.

If you are reading this book, it is because you want to achieve something you haven't yet figured out. Your success begins with the realization of where you are versus where you want to be. Perhaps you need to deal with parts of your past through therapy. Maybe you've been lied to about something so much that you believe it to be true. Maybe you feel that making a decision you feel right about will come with consequences from people close to you.

Perhaps you have a big idea or have already figured out exactly what you want to achieve and are seeking ways to more clearly define how you intend to achieve it. Sometimes people dance around wonderful ideas and just want that one last piece of the puzzle which will help them get to where they need to be. As we move into the BIAS mindset in the next chapter, you will discover the thought process that may give you that last piece. You may even grow beyond your wildest dreams and achieve greatness.

There is nothing more amazing to me than watching someone ultimately realize they have immense value. You, dear reader, have that immense value. I believe you were created for a purpose and that no matter where you are, what you do or what title you hold, there is more in store for you in this life. You *are* special. You *are* unique. You have worth!

You bring something to this world no one else can offer.

Now you need to make a decision:

- Are you going to let the lies of your past remain the truth of your future?
- Are you going to allow your peers, friends and family to make decisions that will ultimately impact *your* life?
- Will a past traumatic event determine what will happen to you years from now?
- Did you make a poor decision years ago that needs to be changed now?
- Will you continue to watch other people earn the promotions or recognition that you feel you deserve?

If you answered no to each of these questions, I think you have made your decision. Now what?

BIAS is the success mindset that will help you achieve all your goals and achieve excellence. Once you've adopted a BIAS mindset in your daily life, everything you do will be driven by a need to live your purpose and achieve major goals you establish for yourself. Life will make more sense. Ralph Waldo Emerson once said, "Once you make a decision, the Universe conspires to make it happen."

What does it mean to decide?

During the first week in January, the gym is full of people who made a decision to get healthier. They made a New Year's resolution with the greatest of ambitions to join a gym. By March, most are nowhere to be found. Why?

Making a decision is more than wishful thinking or having big goals. Deciding on something (making a resolution) must be founded in the belief that a change *must* be made and *can* be made. Without developing a deep understanding of what needs to be changed and why, it is much more likely you will revert to what you are accustomed to. The likelihood of achieving success will then diminish considerably. Without deep understanding and confidence you will succeed, it cannot be a decision; it is merely a hope or wish.

Hope is a feeling of expectation and desire for a certain thing to happen. A wish is a feeling or expressing a strong desire or hope for something not easily attainable. Resolutions are firm decisions to do or not do something.

Do you see the difference? Decisions (resolutions) are based on facts, principles and the exploration of alternatives.

You've examined the facts. There is something you want that you don't currently have. Maybe situations from your past need to be dealt with. Maybe you need to retrain your mind to stop believing in falsehoods. Maybe it's time to create new habits.

Principles and passions create the foundation that will ultimately drive you to do what you do. They will also ultimately help you achieve your goals.

You are already in the process of exploring your alternatives; it's why you picked up this book. What you are doing now isn't working exactly how you had hoped, so you aren't fully reaching success in certain areas of your life.

You have all the tools in place to make a decision. If your goal is to get healthy or lose weight, don't wait until New Year's Day to make that decision; make it now! Your TV won't miss you. Your family will thank you for giving them more years with you. Sitting on the couch won't help you reach that goal. The weight isn't going to magically fall off, so stop wishing for it and *decide*. A dear friend once told me years ago that hope is not a strategy. Your strategy is to do the necessary work and make the decision that will change your life.

Maybe your goal is not to lose weight. If your goal is to have a greater impact in your church or to raise money to help the homeless or to be a more effective boss, the principals are all the same. Regardless of what your goal is, you must first realize you can do something differently and decide what will help you realize success.

When I started working in software renewals, there was a lot I didn't know. I would not have survived in that environment had I chosen not to learn. After three years with that company, I also saw leaders who were spectacular with their teams. My attitude was refreshed. For the first time in my life I wanted to be a leader.

I was eventually offered a job with another company. During the interview process I emphasized that I wanted to be a leader. I was promoted after two years with them, then again 18 months later, then again two years after that. I knew what I wanted and made the *decision* to pursue it with high focus until I had developed the habit of success that would carry me toward my goals.

I have been surrounded by world-class leaders, mentors and coaches. I have been allowed to explore things which get me excited about going to work every day. If it weren't for the leaders at my company, I may not have been afforded an opportunity to discover this part of myself. When you have good leaders in your life, you can be content and excited doing what you do. The right leaders will put you in the right position and encourage you to discover the things that truly make you happy.

Because I have finally experienced outstanding leaders, I know exactly where I want to be if I remain in the corporate world. The driving force behind all my decisions is to help and elevate those around me. I find absolute delight in building teams and helping others be successful. Training others has become one of the most rewarding elements of my job. Raising people to their full potential is what gets me to leap out of bed in the morning.

As a certified business coach and professional speaker, I observe faces in the audience when I get in front of a room and deliver information. I love seeing the ah-ha moment when something I've said resonates with them. When that happens, I know I have helped them make a decision that will bring them to the next stage of their life. For me, it's about engaging my passion for others and helping them understand something about themselves they may not have known. It's the best feeling in the world.

Once you have found your purpose, you can begin doing what you were created to do. There will be no stopping you. You will be able to develop WISE goals and achieve them regularly. Every aspect of your life will start falling into place, and you will find peace and contentment. The best part is that you already have it in you.

When Tanya made the decision to not live in poverty anymore, she found meaning in her life. She now sees other children who have had similar struggles as hers growing up. She connects with them in a way almost no one else can.

She lifts the most downtrodden in her community and has made a name for herself. She provides a voice to the voiceless because she made a decision.

Andrei's father chose to leave Romania and come to the United States. Had it not been for this decision, Andrei would not have had the opportunities to start his own computer business at 10 years old or to become a chief information security officer at 32. The decisions we make have lasting impacts within our lives and in generations to come.

My family chose not to improve their situation. I could have easily handed down this legacy to my children, but I *decided*. I was offered a position to go back to my old career about a year after my new one started, but I made the decision to stay where I was despite financial hardship. That decision changed my life and the lives of my children for the better

You are about to make a decision that can have a lasting impact. It is bigger than you. It's about your family, your community and your country. Your children and their children may very well reap the benefit of the decisions you make today. You can make up for your past mistakes because those mistakes don't define you. They may shape you, but they do not control you. *Decide* right now to have a new life with new goals and new success. It's up to you.

   Success Unleashed: Mastering Your Life's Purpose

Chapter 6
BIAS Mindset

"The meaning of life is to find your gift.
The purpose of life is to give it away."

—Pablo Picasso

"How can I find more meaning and purpose in my life?" This is a question many of us have asked, or at least heard someone else ask in one form or another. According to Lifeway Research, most Americans (57%) say they wonder [this] at least monthly, with more than 1 in 5 saying they consider the question daily (21%) or weekly (21%).[16]

So far, you have learned about different areas of life that compete for your attention and how they can hold you back from reaching your full potential. If you are using what you learn here to advance your career, you may feel overwhelmed if you're facing one or more of those challenges. If you are focused on reaching personal goals, you may also face similar setbacks.

---

16 research.lifeway.com/2021/04/06/americans-views-of-lifes-meaning-and-purpose-are-changing

These setbacks are only amplified if you are not in line with your ultimate purpose. You are unique because your purpose may be different from most or all other people you encounter. This is why social and family pressures can be so extreme. Other people don't have the same life purpose as yours. If they don't understand what purpose *is,* they will have a hard time watching you pursue yours.

In writing this book, I originally wanted to help people develop a mindset for business success. However, during the process I discovered it was so much more. Earlier I explained how to conduct a root cause analysis to identify what makes you happy. That analysis can be aligned with your ultimate purpose. Painter Bob Ross might have called it a "happy little accident." Does this mean your passions are always in line with your purpose or that your purpose always results in a career? No.

Recall that Tanya discovered her purpose was to find those who grew up in similar circumstances and to help them to grow beyond their limitations. She now lifts their mindset out of poverty so they can be equipped to thrive. But she doesn't do this for a living. She is not licensed to practice psychology or early childhood development, nor is she an educator. As we proceed through this chapter, one of the steps we will cover is how to build a goals list. You may discover a common thread to help you to uncover your purpose. It may be something you can monetize, but that won't always be the case.

To develop the right mindset for your life, it is important to discover your purpose. You may not understand it yet, but as you work through these exercises you will be much closer to achieving it.

The BIAS mindset is a process by which you can develop habits that lead to success, and it will condition you to achieve a variety of goals. The more goals you have, the more likely you can discover the common thread between them and your unique purpose. Examine these areas of your life:

Professional	Financial
Personal	Educational
Spiritual	Other
Relationship	

It's very possible you will discover a pattern here. Perhaps that is your ultimate purpose.

Before now, I didn't know what my ultimate purpose was. I was missing *why* I was put on Earth in the first place. I have worked hard to learn what I've needed to know. I have found ways to thrive in various jobs I've had. Despite being good at my work, I have never found fulfillment. Instead, I went through the motions, struggling to make a living doing jobs that weren't really fulfilling. Only in recent years did I find something outside my day job that gave me the sense of fulfillment I've always wanted. I still couldn't understand why it made me so happy.

As I build new goals, I apply these techniques to ensure I am following my purpose. I find myself happier. My work does not feel like work. My stress levels have gone down considerably. I go to bed excited and wake up ready to dive into whatever tasks await me for the day. I am eager to move forward in life because I finally have a clear direction. Does this mean I have a completely stress-free life? No. But stresses caused by purpose-misalignment are almost completely removed.

Imagine that *you* stated that last sentence. How does it

feel? Is it different from what you feel at work? Do you feel this way performing your daily tasks? Read the last paragraph again. Imagine yourself saying those words. Remember the feeling. This can be your life!

Here are some definitions of a BIAS mindset:

> **Bias:** *a disproportionate weight in favor of or against an idea or thing, usually in a way that is closed-minded, prejudicial, or unfair;*
>
> **Mindset:** *the established set of attitudes held by someone;*
>
> **Success:** *the accomplishment of an aim or purpose;*
>
> **Purpose:** *the reason for which something is done or created or for which something exists; and*
>
> **Goal:** *the object of a person's ambition or effort; an aim or desired result*

Obstacles tend to create a certain bias in your habits, attitudes and perceptions of the world around you. These biases can prevent you from moving forward effectively; they may actually move you away. You must understand that what you've done up to this point has not gotten you to your goals, so something will need to change.

By developing a positive bias in your habits, attitudes and perceptions, you will build the momentum you need to reach your goals. You will also begin reforming relationships or building new ones altogether. I've seen many people give up on their goals because of obstacles, unseen opportunities, destructive relationships or a lack of confidence.

As you adopt the BIAS mindset, new opportunities will present themselves to you every day. Eventually you will realize that achieving your goals and living your purpose are

Success Unleashed: Mastering Your Life's Purpose

not myths. You can unlock your purpose and become a better version of yourself by following the steps outlined here.

You will begin developing habits which help you achieve your goals. As you apply the mindset continually over time, you will achieve your goals faster and enjoy the process more. By developing this new habit, you will transform your life in ways you may not have known. Everyone around you will be uplifted because of your success, because these habits tend to rub off on other people. As you succeed so will they.

BIAS is detailed in four parts:

- Build your goals list.
- Instill courage.
- Act boldly.
- Say yes.

Every goal setting technique begins with writing them down. I suggest you avoid anything temporary like sticky notes or lipstick on a mirror, but you should write them. Goals should be written in a permanent location and remain visible to you regularly. If you keep a journal or diary, be sure to go back and read it often. I like to print my goals and hang them on the walls in my office. I make the font large enough to fill an entire page so I can read it from a distance.

According to a study by Dr. Gail Matthews at the Dominican University in California, "You are 42 percent more likely to achieve your goals if you write them down."[17] This is a massive statistic! When combined with other principals of the BIAS mindset, the likelihood of you reaching your goals increases exponentially.

---

17 www.snow.edu/blog/Why_you_should_write_down_your_goals.html

Step one is to build your goals list. When I say build it, I don't mean jot something down on a sticky note so it can fall off your monitor and land behind your desk where you'll never see it again. Let's break down this step word by word so you develop correct habits from the start.

BUILD

According to a Google search, the verb "build" means

1) to construct (something) by putting parts or material together; and

2) to make stronger or more intense.

When I think of constructing something, I think of the time, planning and work that go into that process. Why should building your goals list be any different? It is fitting that it should take time, planning and work. Each goal should involve a decision process. Otherwise, I'd question whether it's really a goal in the first place.

According to UMass Dartmouth, the decision process involves seven steps:

1. Identify the decision (why it needs to be made in the first place).
2. Gather relevant information.
3. Identify the alternatives.
4. Weigh the evidence.
5. Choose among alternatives.
6. Take action.
7. Review your decision and its consequences.

You can find more details at www.umassd.edu/fycm/decision-making/process.

If an organization makes the decision to purchase a new

tool or product, they follow these steps. Why, as individuals, shouldn't we follow a similar process when we determine our goals? This step will take you some time, and you will very likely revisit it often as you work through the next ones along the way. By the time you've completed your list, you'll be proud of the result and have a clear definition of where you want to be in different areas of your life.

YOUR

Our families, friends and colleagues can be very strong forces on us. When we were young, our parents tried to shape and guide us to the best of their ability. As many of us moved on to college or elsewhere, our professors and guidance counselors steered us along a path others took before us. Then we entered the workforce where our bosses guided us toward a proven and successful career path. Our spouses can also have expectations and will often try to push us in one direction or another.

There is a common distinction regarding the above examples: none of them are *your* goals! They are all based on what other people think you should do. Many fail to consider what *you* want to achieve in life. It should be simple to ignore them, but let's be honest. Those very loud voices will not be silenced, and they will always be present.

As you develop your goals list, be sure to include your wants, passions, desires and hopes. Other people may guide you, but the decision to choose a path ultimately belongs to you. It is tragic when people do what others tell them to do despite having no passion for it.

I recently heard a story about a young man whose parents insisted he go to law school. He didn't want to study law, but he didn't want to disappoint his parents; so he went anyway. He was miserable the entire time. His grades were good enough to get him through the program, but his heart was never in it. His real purpose in life was to help others learn and achieve physical fitness. He wanted nothing more than to be a physical education teacher and coach. Because of the pressure applied to him by his family, he was nowhere close to that goal.

During his senior year of college, he decided to take a risk. He dropped law school and pursued a degree in physical education and kinesiology. He graduated with top honors and became a personal trainer and physical education teacher and coach. When he told his parents about his accomplishment, they told him the only thing they were disappointed with was how he had felt so much shame in following his passion.

As you develop your goals it is important you follow your passion. This will not always lead to new careers, promotions or wealth beyond your wildest expectations. In fact, some passions will not change our lifestyles at all. However, by following our passions and achieving goals, we'll gain confidence, discover joy and gain the mental endurance we need to achieve more goals and follow other passions that may actually lead to career success.

Not all passions are prudent for your career. One of the best things we can do for ourselves is to apply wisdom to each of our decisions. While becoming a rock star drummer in my mid-40s sounds like fun, it would not be wise to think I could actually begin that career and have the abil-

     Success Unleashed: Mastering Your Life's Purpose

ity to support my family. I enjoy making music, but it is not prudent for me to pursue it professionally since I've already established myself in other areas. By examining your decisions and the promise each of them holds, you will be able to determine if it's better for your career or your mental health to follow that passion.

Regardless of how your goal achievement manifests in your life, my hope is that you will discover your purpose. Once you've done that, any goals not in alignment with that purpose will distract you from true happiness and fulfillment. Develop *your* goals. Follow *your* passions. Live *your* life. No one else gets to live it, so you might as well do it right.

GOALS

In the next chapter we will discuss WISE goals. You may have heard of SMART goals which were developed by George Doran, Arthur Miller and James Cunningham. They wrote an article in 1981 called, *There's a SMART Way to Write Management Goals and Objectives.*[18] These goals are Specific, Measurable, Attainable, Relevant and Timely. The SMART goal method has become a global standard for goal setting. It is fantastic for setting what I call "next step" goals and can be applied to WISE goals when you break them into bite-sized chunks. SMART goals are often used by companies to achieve their goals, but they are not always applicable to our life goals.

As you develop each goal, I encourage you to aim high. Real high. These goals should be so high that they don't feel

---

18 community.mis.temple.edu/mis0855002fall2015/files/2015/10/S.M.A.R.T-Way-Management-Review.pdf

attainable. In his book, *Good to Great,* Jim Collins coined the term BHAG which stands for Big, Hairy, Audacious Goals.

When President Kennedy announced the mission to the moon in 1960, it had never been done or even considered. We had barely made it out of our atmosphere at that point. Kennedy said we would land a man on the moon by the end of the decade. The problem was that no one had any idea how to accomplish that. Kennedy's declaration rallied the support of the country and set the tone for the government to bankroll the massive undertaking so we as a nation could achieve that astronomical goal. This is a great example of a BHAG.

The moon landing goal was time sensitive. This should not be a factor when setting your own goals. Why would we remove the time aspect?

Several years ago, I set a goal to win first place in a weight-loss challenge. I joined a gym and for the next 90 days worked maniacally to be number one. During those three months, I lost 46 pounds and 8 inches around my waist. Every aspect of my health improved during that challenge, and the people who saw me consistently commented on how much I had changed in a very short period.

I did not win the contest. I didn't even place. My goal was to win. By not winning it removed my drive to continue. I've since gained back all 46 of those pounds (and more). One of my current goals is to live a healthier life, achieve a sustainable weight and maintain healthy reports from my doctor. I want to be able to continue helping others reach their goals and to guide my daughters through adulthood and parenthood. I would also love to watch my grandchildren grow up.

　　　　Success Unleashed: Mastering Your Life's Purpose

You should not include a time-sensitive aspect with WISE goals because the objective is for you to reach your goal. We will help you understand your *why* so you will have a well-defined value in mind.

LIST

You will have goals in many areas of your life that you work toward simultaneously. It may sound challenging, but you are already a multi-dimensional person regularly engaged in many different activities. By understanding goals in each area, you will speed up the process of building success habits. Some goals will be achieved relatively fast, while others may take more time. Some will be much easier than you originally thought, and others will take years to achieve. You will be challenged throughout all this.

As you begin to succeed, you will want success more and more. You will find opportunities to set new goals beyond ones you have met. This process can be repeated indefinitely, and you will continue to get better each time. You will unleash your excellence. The more you practice this new habit, the more ingrained it will become in your mind. Eventually it will be a normal and natural process rather than something you might otherwise attribute to luck.

By following the BIAS mindset, you will eventually make it your normal process. It is a process that takes time and work, so it may not come naturally or easily. You will get frustrated at times, and you may sometimes want to quit along the way. It will be hard but ultimately worth it. Trust this process and learn to enjoy the journey.

As you develop a BIAS mindset, you will eventually look

back and realize how much you've grown (written records will help). The process gets easier with time, so don't give up on yourself. You are worth the work. You are worth the effort. Your family is worth going through this process, too. They will love the outcome so long as you follow your purpose.

Chapter 7
WISE Goals

*"If you don't know where you are going,
you will probably end up somewhere else."*

—Lawrence J. Peter

If you've ever read a personal development book, listened to a keynote speaker, heard a podcast or listened to a broadcaster who is invested in the growth of others, you are familiar with goal setting. Why do so many people talk about it? The answer is simple: not enough people do it.

Establishing proper goals is foundational to any success principle. Earlier, we covered SMART goals, one of the most popular and highly effective goal setting methods. Not all goals can be designed in this manner, though. In work settings, leaders will often use Key Performance Indicators (KPIs) or Objectives and Key Results (OKRs).

Despite the offerings of techniques, approaches, methods and gimmicks for developing goals lists, very few of them go into much detail. There are key points you need to be aware of, but I have found very few that provide clear instruction on how to fully develop goals from start to finish.

Most goal setting methods follow the same general patterns about being concise, specific, memorable, accountable, etc. Some even provide statistics that reinforce why each step is so important. You have probably heard enough of these statistics to make your head spin. The WISE goal setting method described in this chapter is a prescriptive guide about how to develop your goals so that all statistics fall into place.

WISE goals follow three primary principles of goal setting: root cause analysis, subconscious programming, and accountability. These principles will help with writing your goals list and reinforcing them into your subconscious mind.

Root Cause Analysis

In WISE, the "W" stands for Why. Why is your goal your goal?

WISE goals begin with the 5 Whys technique developed by Sakichi Toyoda in the 1930s. It was originally designed to function within manufacturing to discover why equipment failed or why bottlenecks occurred. The same principle still applies when developing your goals.

In 2023, I tried to create a WISE goal that would help me become a Chief Artificial Intelligence Officer (CAIO). AI was gaining momentum within the IT community, and similar tech tools began to dot the landscape. Technology companies raced to see who could incorporate AI and machine learning into their offerings so they wouldn't be left behind.

Because I also wanted to be on the executive team of a company, I set another goal that was fueled by my passion to help others grow and succeed. At that time I was a sales leader, but a head sales position didn't really appeal to me. My sales approach was more client-success oriented, so a Chief Customer Officer (CCO) position appealed to my personality.

My career coach and I applied the WISE goal setting method first to the CAIO position. I listed my goal as of that moment, then asked my 5 whys. The deeper I made it through the process, the closer I got to the real reason I wanted that goal.

Let's use an example related to day-to-day behavior—speeding on the highway. If you were pulled over for speeding on the highway, you could analyze what led to you speeding in the first place. Perhaps it was because you stayed up too late watching a movie the night before. It's not that you're necessarily a bad driver; you were trying to be responsible after having made a decision that created a chain reaction.

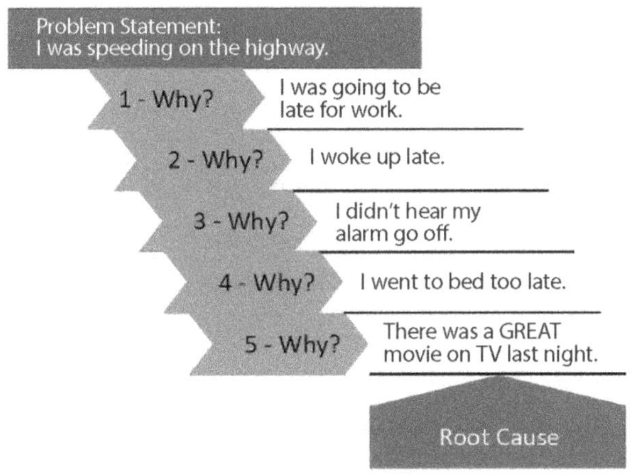

There can be a challenge with the 5 Whys. When we try to apply this to our life goals, we tend to display a bias. We answer in a way that directly supports the goal we have set for ourselves. It is critical to have someone else (perhaps two or three people) listen to your answers. They can help you answer in more detail at each step. My team has developed a WISE workshop. We break participants into small groups and encourage them to go beyond asking why and to truly seek understanding before proceeding to the next level.

When I applied this technique to my CAIO goal, I discovered the goal was not in line with my root cause. The deeper I got, the more I realized I was merely seeking a senior position out of curiosity about technology. It did not align with my core values or purpose.

I then switched to the CCO goal and discovered it was in perfect alignment with my root cause of wanting to help people. As CCO I would have the ability and responsibility to create conditions favorable to my customers' needs. I would also be able to guide, mentor and inspire those within the organization to be the best versions of themselves. This would give me the ability to create a culture where people could leverage their skills, develop new ones, be themselves and help their customers, all with a great level of freedom.

In the end, a CCO position would give me the ability to influence many more people than I could ever reach on my own. I will have completed this goal while simultaneously helping unleash excellence in others.

As you go through the WISE process, understand your goals may need to be adjusted. You may discover more about yourself than you realize, and that might challenge you to reevaluate the goals you initially set. For example, writing this book stemmed from my original keynote address which

 Success Unleashed: Mastering Your Life's Purpose

focused on career advancement. As I did more research, I uncovered some of the principles woven throughout the book. I eventually had to shift my goal. I went from helping others advance their careers to helping them identify their own unique purpose. I returned to root cause analysis and discovered my answers were not where they had originally been. This allowed me to change the goal, and this book wrote itself.

When you write down your goals, you are 42% more likely to achieve them. By following through with root cause analysis and writing down the questions, answers and root cause, you will solidify the foundation of your goal. You will be much more likely to achieve it because you will understand it better at the root level.

Subconscious Programming

Have you ever had an idea that was there for a second and gone the next? Unfortunately, it happens to all of us. The conscious mind has a tremendous number of things to focus on in any given moment. Ideas can be very short lived. The same can be said for goals. You have learned that writing goals down gives you a much higher likelihood of reaching them. The written goal can serve as a permanent record of what your goals have been.

As with conscious thoughts, goals can and do go by the wayside as more thoughts and ideas intrude into your daily life. And, if the written goal is not placed in a location you see regularly and access easily, there's a good chance it will get placed on a bookshelf, fall behind your desk, get erased or discarded by some other means.

Our subconscious minds are extremely powerful, especially when ideas are deeply ingrained. According to Dr. Bruce Lipton, biologist and author of *Biology of Belief,* the subconscious mind is 500,000 times more powerful than the conscious mind.[19] Your mind cannot differentiate between the past, present or future. If you can successfully program your subconscious mind that your goal is your future reality, it will do everything possible to make that happen. If we want to achieve our goals, we need to program our subconscious minds to believe we have already achieved them.

In WISE, the "I" stands for Imagine. When you are able to imagine how life will be once you've attained your goal, your brain will begin to think it is your new reality. In her book, *The Secret,* Rhonda Byrne does a fantastic job explaining the mental phenomenon of visualization and how it impacts the events in our live. Without this subconscious step, the chances of achieving your goal are inversely reduced by a factor of 500,000

"S" stands for Specify every detail. This works alongside Imagine. When you imagine your future, it is important to involve all your senses. Your subconscious mind will use more hard wiring to draw that picture in your head when you involve more senses. Eventually, you want this vision to be so extremely detailed that you could draw or paint from memory an image of your future. This will take a lot of practice and regular meditation on your goal. When you create a daily habit of focusing on your goals with this level of detail, it will create a crystal-clear vision of your future.

---

19 www.vitalityunleashed.com.au/the-power-of-your-subconscious-mind-2

One of my life goals is to live healthier than I was in the past. It would have been fun to go through this exercise with Voodoo Doughnut. How ironic. Imagine being a fly on the wall when founders Kenneth "Cat Daddy" Pogson and Tres Shannon were brainstorming Voodoo Doughnut back in 2000.[20] They joked about their ambition to achieve world doughnut domination, but there had to be much talk about the details. They must have imagined bright colors (or lack thereof) and decor inside their stores, the ingredients and tools they would use to create the doughnuts, the cloyingly sweet smell of the kitchens, the way their shoes would stick to the floors as they traversed between the kitchen and front counter, and anything else which would create the vibe for customers.

They must have thought of flavor combinations, colors, smells and textures, how customers would react, where they would be located, how they would market this crazy idea and what tools they would use. While brainstorming this idea, they were bound to involve all their senses along with a business plan. Since their initial launch, Voodoo Doughnut has established locations in 19 states as of 2023 and has established themselves as one of the most unique doughnut shops ever created.

What is your goal? Do you want to be CEO of a major company, open a dance studio, become a best-selling author or patent a series of inventions that will change humanity? How will people respond to you when they encounter you? What does the chair in your office feel like? What does the

____

20 www.voodoodoughnut.com/the-voodoo-doughnut-story

studio smell like? What recognition will you receive and from whom? What will your bank account look like? How will your spouse, partner, children, parents and co-workers treat you? What kind of clothes will you wear? What does your food taste like? Where will you live? How many countries will you visit? How will you feel physically and emotionally? What will you do for recreation at this stage of life?

The more detail you can provide yourself and the more senses you include, the more your subconscious mind will see it as reality. Once this happens, everything you do, everywhere you go and everyone with whom you interact will begin showing you opportunities that point you toward the achievement of your goals. The opportunities are already there; you likely cannot see them because your subconscious mind is looking elsewhere.

The more explicit the vision, the more you will be amazed by your mind's ability to identify where your new life will be. You cannot resist it, and you won't be able to stop it. Your subconscious mind is too powerful for your conscious mind to overcome.

Does this mean life will look exactly as you now imagine once you achieve your goals? Not necessarily. Some goals will have a far more significant impact on your life than you could ever expect. Every day might be a *pinch me, I'm dreaming* moment. In other cases, we may come to realize the goal we had is not quite that magnificent.

Maybe you have the impression that all CEOs live in mansions and fly around in private jets. If you become a CEO of a small organization, you may discover you'll still fly coach, drive a modest car and live in the same home you have today. It doesn't mean you failed, though. It simply means you might still be in the process of growing toward the point where you will have all the things you imagined. You might also realize certain material things you imagined are not needed for fulfillment or happiness. Regardless, once you achieve your goal, make a new one and keep going.

Accountability

In WISE, the "E" stands for Evangelize your goal. Tell everyone! What is the good in having a goal if you never have the satisfaction of reaching it?

Throughout my life I've had different methods of goal setting. I prided myself on remembering what my goals were, so I didn't write them down. That never amounted to anything. There is truth in the saying, "The dullest pencil is better than the sharpest mind." However, once I did write down my goals, I would either put them in a notebook and never open it again or set them on my desk where it would eventually fall off and be forgotten. At least I had engaged one more sense for establishing goals, but I should have kept them in front of me.

My wife teases me because I live by the calendar on my phone. I often say, "If it's not on my calendar, it isn't happening." I've trained myself to use the Notepad app on my laptop and on my phone to remind myself of my goals. I also list them in a Tasks section of my email program. For goals with time requirements, I use phone alerts to remind me of my progress.

If I write down my goal and leave it on the dashboard of my car, the only people who ever know about it will be those who ride with me. Likewise, if I stick one to the mirror in my master bathroom, the only people who will know about it are my wife and me (unless I have some very comfortable house guests).

There are three types of people to whom you will tell your goals, and they are all important. Telling others your goals will involve some courage, but you will absolutely not regret taking this step.

The three types of people you will encounter are:
- people who don't care;
- people who tell you that you'll never reach your goal; and
- people who will support you every step of the way.

You must get through all the people who don't care before you ever get to anything else. For every hundred people you tell, 96 won't give a second thought about your goals. Three of them will be negative, and only one (two if you're lucky) will be in your corner. You must get through those 96 people first, so start right away; then get to the other four. The first 96 who don't care are neutrals. You may eventually be able to turn neutrals into positives, but work must be done first.

Believe it or not, you actually need the negative people. They can still help you achieve your goals. We all know someone (perhaps ourselves) who performs best when told by others they *can't* do something.

Tell your family, friends, colleagues, church, bowling team, their families, and start going through your phone contacts of people you haven't seen in ten years. After you've told everyone you know, you will eventually find someone so negative it might make you physically sick. They will tell you all the reasons why you can't achieve your goal. You lack the right education. You're not the right height. You vote the wrong way. You have no authority to do what you think you're going to do. Most businesses fail; why should yours succeed? You don't dress well enough. Your car isn't fancy enough. You live in the wrong neighborhood. Whatever!

You will encounter people who come up with every reason in the world why you will never achieve your goal, but you've learned something they haven't. The subconscious mind is 500,000 times more powerful than the conscious mind.

These people can be tough to listen to, but there is a way to steer their comments toward your success. Your conscious mind will want to agree with them as they spew their reasoning at you, but hold firm *knowing* you will reach your goal. They might even point out something you may have overlooked which you can use to your advantage.

Maybe you do need to think about something differently. Maybe you need to understand the demographics better in your target location. Maybe you need to get in better touch with the age group you want to engage with. There are always areas in which to improve, so take the opportunity to learn from negative people who enlighten you about how to think more effectively.

Maybe this person is a former high school rival who thinks the rivalry is still going. This is your chance to show them what real success looks like. You have the chance to really shine and show this negative individual how great you really are. People have no right to tell you that you are less than them. You have already succeeded in whatever you set out to achieve. They can't stop you because it has already happened in your subconscious mind. They can only look at you with admiration once you've achieved it.

After you have gotten through two or three negative motivators, you will find the positive people. These are your cheerleaders and accountability partners. Accountability partners will be positive but at times may behave like neutrals. This is okay. They aren't negative but do care about your success, though they may be less vocal about it than the cheerleaders.

Cheerleaders believe in your vision so much that they will stay awake at night thinking about what your success will look like. They will call you in the middle of your workday to ask how things are going. They will call you, email you and text you whenever they think of you. You will get calls at 2 am because they need to know how you're doing and how far you've come toward your goal.

Both negative and positive people will get into your head. They will occupy your mental real estate, and you want them there. You must remember to program your subconscious to realize negative people are wrong and that you have already achieved your goal. Positive people are right, and they will need a progress report.

Your brain will need to show results for both groups. Show the negatives where they went wrong. Don't delay your goal, because the positives are going to hold you accountable. Your subconscious mind will push you toward your goal whether you think you are ready or not. It's your time to shine, and something unbelievable is going to happen. You will begin reaching your goals!

So what's next? Another goal, of course. Only this time, it's going to look a little different.

    Success Unleashed: Mastering Your Life's Purpose

Because you were able to easily achieve your first goal faster than you realized, the negative people will begin to believe in you. Most will stay negative if that's how their minds are wired, but they may become neutral. If you're lucky, they might even become positive. Some of the neutrals will notice you achieved something they vaguely remember you saying a few years ago. Some will become solid cheerleaders as you achieve more of your goals.

The more you succeed, the more people will begin to align themselves with you. People like to be around winners and successful people. You will find that the original 96 people you had to get through becomes lower and lower. The negatives you hear will not be so harsh. The positives will grow, and you will eventually have groupies who are inspired by you and start taking notes on how you achieved your goals. They will start asking you questions about how you reached them, and they will tell you about theirs. This is your opportunity to pay it forward and help them reach their goals.

There are two other types of people you will need to work with. The first three we discussed are your general audience. As you develop your network you will identify specific people who can help you in different ways. Rather than simply cheerleading or trying to hold you back, the next two types will work alongside you.

Mentors

As you learned earlier, mentors are particularly good when you are starting out. They have likely been where you are now and have tips and ideas that can help you push toward your goals. They can provide you with information and shortcut your learning process. They can assign you tasks and projects that will help you develop skills and habits necessary for success.

Because you are pursuing *your* purpose, your mentor will not always be aligned with everything you need from start to finish. You may even outgrow your mentor along the way. Growing your network will allow you to understand who among you are equipped to take you from one level to the next. You must continue building your network so you can continue to grow.

It's okay if you outgrow your mentors. In healthy mentoring relationships, they will help you with a transition to another mentor who can take you to the next level. Your former mentors can now become your cheerleaders because they have a vested interest in your ongoing success.

The more goals you set, the more mentors you will need. I have a friend who is one of the strongest leaders I've ever met. She is empathetic, compassionate, organized and incredibly insightful. During one of the most difficult years of my life, she stood beside me and allowed me to vent when I needed to. She would then offer me suggestions on how I could deal with situations that caused me the most difficulty. She continues to be one of my closest friends and occasionally checks in with me to see how I'm doing.

I use different mentors when dealing with my marriage and my finances, even for writing this book. As much as I love and trust my friend, she is not equipped to advise on the experiences I've had in these other areas. I found other mentors whose expertise is better suited for those.

Study your goals list and compare it to your network.

     Success Unleashed: Mastering Your Life's Purpose

Who do you know with a higher understanding than yours in a certain area? Whose success would you like to replicate?

Coaches

While mentors give you information you didn't have before, coaches draw information and solutions out from you.

You are smarter than you realize. When faced with a challenge, you may have a solution, but sometimes you need someone to draw it out of you. Coaches are often trained professionals, so you may wish to hire a coach rather than simply draw from your network. Coaches will take the time to learn how you think and where your strengths are. They will ask targeted questions which help you arrive at conclusions and solutions on your own.

Coaches come in many different flavors I recommend you do some research before hiring a coach to make sure that you get the most value out of your investment. According to *Artists in Business,* there are 20 different types of coaching commonly available in the market:[21]

Business	Holistic
Life	Performance
Executive	Mental Health
Career	Communication
Sales	Intuitive
Relationship Group	Leadership Development
Skills	Targeted Behavioral
Success	Legacy
Transformational Team	Newly Assigned Leader

I've hired several coaches in my life. As I look toward my

---

21 artistsinbusiness.com/coaching/types

current goals, I know I will hire several others in the future. Coaches have drawn out fantastic results in my ability to deal with difficult situations like empathetically firing underperforming employees, creating company-changing solutions to ongoing problems, and more. To learn the skills coaches have drawn out of me would have taken years longer without them. In fact, I might have never found a solution at all.

Trust is the most important element in both coaching and mentoring relationships. Boundaries and clear expectations need to be established up front. When working with a professional it is important to document those boundaries. As with any relationship, it will take time for trust to be fully developed, so you will need to exercise patience. Also understand that trust flows in both directions. If you are untrustworthy with your mentor or coach, they may terminate the relationship, so it's best to err on the side of honesty and transparency.

Both mentoring and coaching relationships must remain confidential at all times. They are also different from therapy, so be careful not to blur the lines into your mental health. By agreeing to confidentiality you will be encouraging more trust between you, and that will allow for more effective sessions.

WISE goals are powerful. The more you dive into this process, the better off you will be. If you take the time to truly understand each of your goals on a subconscious level, no force can prevent you from achieving it.

Use the following worksheet to write down your WISE goals and the underlying reasons for them. You can also find this worksheet at www.thedashlegacy.net/downloads.

Use this for each of your goals to have a clear path for achieving them. Eventually you'll be able to use this to define your ultimate purpose.

Goal Category	Goal	Reason
Professional		
Personal		
Spiritual		
Relational		
Financial		
Educational		
Other		

WISE goals:

W: ____

   1) _______________________________________

   2) _______________________________________

   3) _______________________________________

   4) _______________________________________

   5) _______________________________________

I: ____

S: ____

E: ____

Chapter 8
Courage

*"I learned that courage was not the absence of fear,
but the triumph over it. The brave man is not he who
does not feel afraid, but he who conquers that fear."*

—Nelson Mandela

In chapter six we outlined what it means to have a BIAS mindset.

- Build your goals list.
- Instill courage.
- Act boldly.
- Say yes.

After you have taken the time to build your goals list and gone through the work of setting WISE goals, it's time to move into the next step of the BIAS mindset: Instill Courage.

If you have built your goals big enough, there's a good chance you're experiencing some fear right now. This is a completely natural feeling, and it will require some degree of courage to take the next step.

Before we dive in, let's discuss the effects of fear and anxiety. Fear is a physical, chemical response within your body. It's not all in your head, though your head has a lot to do with it.

According to Northwestern Medicine, when you experience fear, stress hormones like cortisol and adrenaline are released.[22] Your blood pressure and heart rate increase. You start breathing faster. Even your blood flow changes. Blood actually flows away from your heart and into your limbs, making it easier for you to start throwing punches or run for your life. Excessive cortisol (stress hormone) in your body causes all sorts of medical issues, including weight gain (retains fat), increased blood pressure, diabetes and immune issues. You tend to get sick easier.

Fear will always be a part of our lives, so it is important to acknowledge it when it presents itself and take appropriate steps to manage it. What you'll discover in this chapter is that you don't have to treat worry and anxiety with the reverence you may be treating it with now. In fact, there are methods to overcome anxiety issues and the long-term impacts of stress.

Mel Robbins has done extensive research on fear and anxiety. She explains how it affects the body in her book, *5 Second Rule*. Her conversational approach makes it an easy read, and the content is extraordinary. She was able to overcome her own anxiety issues through the steps outlined in her book.

In 2023, I was challenged to develop my first full-length keynote speech. I have been involved in public speaking for many years, so getting on stage was not a fear for me. However, developing that much content for an audience of pro-

---

22 nm.org/healthbeat/healthy-tips/emotional-health/5-things-you-never-knew-about-fear

fessional speakers was still intimidating. I was not afraid, but it did start an avalanche of events that generated a lot of fear.

After the keynote, I received quite a bit of feedback I could use to make the presentation better. One of my coaches pulled me aside and talked to me about next steps. He advised I should first form a company. I had never worked for myself before. I've always had the safety net of a job to fall back on.

The idea of starting a business effectively removed that safety net. If I followed through with this suggestion, any failure or success would be 100% my fault. All sorts of questions were running through my mind: How would I find new bookings? How would I manage my taxes? What if I wasn't as good as my friends thought I was? What if I succeeded?

My coach then suggested I get a book published before my first paid keynote. I succeeded in taking that step; but at the time, I had already been booked to give my first presentation for an outside organization. This meant I had about four months to write the manuscript and allow enough time to get it edited, designed, published and printed. My writing deadline was only six weeks.

I had already accepted the challenge of starting my own business which was successfully launched in January 2024. I now had the task of developing this content. Did I mention I still had a full-time career, was involved in multiple volunteer organizations and also had a family to take care of?

The little time I had available was disappearing as I considered this adventure, and the fear continued to build. What if this was all for nothing? What would I want my business to look like? What if no one read my book? *What if, what if, what if…*

The late Dr. Susan Jeffers was widely regarded as the queen of self-help, which was quite an accomplishment during the generation in which she lived. She sold millions of copies of her books, winning a Caldecott Honor and becoming a *New York Times* bestselling illustrator. According to her website, "She helped millions of people throughout the world learn to overcome their fears, to heal their relationships and to live with confidence and love."[23] In 1984, Jeffers wrote the international best seller, *Feel the Fear and Do It Anyway,* which put her psychology training and knowledge into an easily digestible format. If you haven't read the book, I strongly recommend it,

Dr. Jeffers highlights in her book that everyone experiences fear. What we choose to do with that fear makes all the difference in the world. It can help us take action instead of being stopped by it. Fear of the unknown (worry) holds back so many people. We imagine many kinds of outcomes. Subsequently, we fail to even take the first step toward reaching our goals.

Fear begins in the amygdala, the area of the brain responsible for decision-making and instincts. It is adaptable, which allows us to continuously learn about our environments. It is also responsible for emotional responses such as fear and anxiety.

In the early stages of human development, people faced real dangers like lions, bears, snakes, etc. If you were hiking on a trail and came across a grizzly bear, it would be appropriate for you to have fear in that moment, but it would be foolish to face that fear and move toward the bear.

---

23 www.susanjeffers.com/about

What about imagined fears? For example, what would your boss say if you asked for a raise? When we think about situations like this, many of us fall into "analysis paralysis." We worry about what the boss will say. We mentally go through many possible outcomes. We work ourselves into a self-defeating state of mind where we think we'll get fired just for asking for a raise, so we never ask for it in the first place.

Maybe you're the best performer on your team but haven't had a raise in years. If you ask, your boss might realize you deserve more money, and maybe they could give you more than you expect. If you acknowledge your worry and simply ask the question, you will have conquered your fear and could end up with a much better outcome than you hoped. Or… they could tell you no and move on with their day.

Either way, you know where you stand, what the outcome is, and you don't stress yourself to the point where your job is no longer enjoyable. It doesn't feel good to be denied a raise, but the longer you spend in a state of stress the more negative the impact will be on your health. Better to just get it over with. Just rip the Band-aid off.

Worrying is normal. A few years ago, my wife was in the hospital for a surgical procedure. I had faith all would be well. After 30 minutes in the operating room, the surgeon came out and asked me to join her for a consultation. They had found cancer cells in my wife's lymphatic system, so they had to stop the operation.

There I was, unexpectedly informed that my wife had stage 3 cancer. Immediately, worry took center stage. What would I do if I lost my wife? How would I raise my kids without her? How could I manage my household without her there to help? I wouldn't be able to go downtown every day for work anymore, so what would I do for work?

Some situations are truly terrifying. Some careers demand it—military, fire fighters, police, rodeo clowns, etc. They are all trained to run toward danger when everyone else is running away. Does that mean they don't feel fear? No. Marines, for example, are told to run toward gunfire. They experience true life-and-death exposure in those moments. Firefighters know they could end up in situations they can't get out of when entering a burning building.

When a police officer approaches a crime scene or stops a car in traffic, they never know what they are going to face, and it could turn life-threatening in an instant. Rodeo clowns run toward aggressive, dangerous bulls to protect a thrown rider from getting trampled. They risk getting trampled themselves or stabbed by the bull's horns.

Be a change agent. Rather than letting problems come to them, Marines put pressure on the enemy so they can dominate the battlefield. You may never face life or death decisions, but what if you adopted this mentality when worry creeps into your head?

Having an attitude like this could make the difference between you remaining stagnant in your life and career or getting the job, promotion or opportunity you've always dreamed of. Maybe you'll move to the location you've always wanted to live. Maybe you'll finally get a date with the man or woman you've been afraid to approach.

Instilling courage does not mean your fears will go away. This is about how you process information and the decision you make to act on something. It starts by acknowledging you have fear, cataloging why you have that feeling and using the information to take appropriate action. Fear is natural. We all have it, and it's there for a reason. Worry, doubt and anxiety are caused by chemical reactions in the brain, but they are otherwise imaginary.

Parents have moments of fear as their children develop— the first time their child spends the night at a friend's house; the day their child gets a driver's license and leaves the house in the car for the first time; the day kids go off to college or join the military. Parents fear the first time their children travel by themselves far from home. My oldest daughter took her first international school trip without us before she turned 18. It was a major challenge for my wife and me.

Think about how much our kids develop in these moments. They learn independence, responsibility, maturity and culture. They begin to understand what parents provide for them and must learn to solve problems independently. It's truly exciting for them as well as the parents.

There are, of course, occasions when fear is reasonable such as when a child breaks a bone that requires setting or surgery. It's also valid when a family member gets serious news from the doctor or when we get a phone call from the police. While there may be growth in moments like these, more serious events go beyond imagined worry and anxiety. This is why we must first categorize the fear we feel and determine if it is legitimate before we choose to act on that fear.

In *5 Second Rule,* Mel Robbins explained that "Excitement and fear [are] the exact same thing in your body. It's just what your brain calls it." When we experience fear, worry and doubt, the first thing you can do to change your attitude is to simply call it excitement. *I'm excited that my son spent the night at his friend's house! I'm excited that my daughter is traveling to another country to learn about their culture and deepen her understanding of the language! I'm excited that my wife kicked cancer's butt!*

By acknowledging you feel fear and reclassifying it as excitement, you will be able to take your first step toward your goals. This will look to everyone else like courage, and maybe it is. You will be instilling courage in yourself. Before you know it, those Big Hairy Audacious Goals you set for yourself will soon be within reach.

Chapter 9
Action

Many years ago, I attended a national event that was packed with superstars. It was called "Get Motivated," and the stage was graced by the likes of General Colin Powell, Zig Ziglar and former First Lady Laura Bush. It was one of the most incredible speaking lineups I'd ever had the opportunity to behold. Nearly 20 years later, I still remember some of the topics covered in those speeches. One particular speech stuck with me more than the rest. The speaker was legendary pro football Hall of Fame member and Super Bowl champion, Joe Montana.

What I recall from Montana's speech was his history with wide receiver Jerry Rice. Montana recalled that when Rice joined the team, he didn't behave like other wide receivers he had played with. At every practice before a game, Rice would run his pass route. When the ball was thrown to him, he would catch it and immediately sprint to the end zone. This was odd during practice because normally a wide receiver would catch the ball and simply go back to the line to get ready for the next drill. Not Rice. He would run his route, catch the ball, then sprint to the end zone.

Run the route, catch the ball, sprint to the end zone. Other receivers mocked him. Even the quarterbacks and coaches didn't understand. When the other players on the team asked Rice why he did this, his response was that the object was to score a touchdown during the game. *Run the route, catch the ball, sprint to the end zone.*

In his first game with the San Francisco 49ers, Rice caught four passes that amounted to 67 yards.[24] During his rookie season, he averaged 18.9 yards per catch, received 49 passes for 927 yards and scored 3 touchdowns. During his second year, he earned the attention of nearly every football fan by catching an amazing 86 passes, and he led the league with 1,570 yards and 15 touchdowns. This would be the first of 11 consecutive 1,000-yard seasons.

It didn't take long for Joe Montana and the rest of the team to realize that Rice was on to something. Shortly after Rice's debut, it became common practice for every wide receiver to sprint to the end zone when they caught the ball during practice. Eventually, all receivers sprinted toward the end zone. *Run the route, catch the ball, sprint to the end zone.* This eventually evolved into *run the route and defend the ball carrier while sprinting to the end zone.*

---

24 www.profootballhof.com/players/jerry-rice

Rice became famous for his quote, "Today I do what others won't, so tomorrow I will do what others can't." Although he was mocked by his teammates for his habit of expecting to score every time he caught the football, he continued to Act Boldly. That eventually led to seven seasons paired with Joe Montana, and they ultimately connected for 55 touchdowns together. His willingness to face criticism and go against the grain was what made him successful. As of 2023, Jerry Rice was still the most decorated and accomplished wide receiver in NFL history. He changed the game of football for all time because he was willing to do what everyone before him was not.

As you build a BIAS mindset, there will be times you are tempted to take the easy way rather than the right way. This temptation will sound appealing, and it is exactly what prevents an overwhelming percentage of people from reaching their goals. In these moments you have an opportunity to make a difficult decision that will give you the most opportunity to grow.

By now you have built your WISE goals list and are telling yourself you feel excitement rather than fear. This has allowed you to Instill Courage. It's time to act on that courage. It's time to Act Boldly!

Four-time world weightlifting champion Jerzy Gregorek struggled with alcohol abuse as an adolescent under communist oppression in Poland during the 1970s and 1980s. He eventually discovered weightlifting and boldly made the decision to replace his alcohol usage with weights. He credits this decision for saving his life.[25] We can apply his simple quote to our lives: "Easy choices, hard life. Hard choices, easy life."

It is easy to fall into the trap of substance abuse, and it can be extremely difficult to overcome. When removing a vice, it is easy to regress into the same patterns that got you there in the first place if that vice is not immediately substituted for something else you want. Shifting habits is hard. The only way to retreat from substances, bad habits or behaviors in favor of good habits and behaviors is to Act Boldly. Pay no attention to the forces (cravings, people, environments) that allow the bad behaviors to be fed.

Recently, I had the opportunity to interview a young woman who had made choices in her life that were not easy. "Renee" grew up in a very small California town that was built on agriculture. Her parents had immigrated to the United States and had almost no formal education. They were able to survive using the skills they had learned in their previous country, but they wanted more for their children. This town had a teen pregnancy rate of over 70%. The nearest college was located over an hour away from where she lived. Her parents wanted a better life for her, so they sacrificed as much as they could and paid for her community college. They wanted her to earn a degree so she could live better than they had.

Renee became an avid STEM (Science, Technology, Engineering and Mathematics) student. She earned a Bachelor of Science in physics and made the choice to stay in school to pursue a PhD in molecular biophysics. During our interview I asked Renee why she was so driven to study such

---

25 scottkujak.com/the-happy-body-and-olympic-weightlifting-with-jerzy-gregorek

a difficult subject and what she hoped to do with it during her professional life. She told me she wanted to improve the lives of people who had been subjected to a specific disease. Her education during her doctoral studies has given her the tools to do what no one else on the planet has ever been able to accomplish.

Renee made the decision to do what no member of her family or community had done before. Her decision to Act Boldly changed the course of her family legacy. It is entirely probable that one day she will be awarded the Nobel Prize for physics, medicine or chemistry.

As with facing your fears, bold action will take courage. You will encounter people who do not believe you are capable of doing what you set out to accomplish, and some will not be shy about it. These naysayers can be parents, siblings, close friends, colleagues or even spouses. To achieve your goals, you will face adversity. As frightening as that sounds, it will open the door for engagement with people who will be your biggest cheerleaders.

When we see goals in front of us and fail to act, we develop the habit of inaction. This causes us to build ourselves into a glass prison in which we feel powerless to get where we want. I have seen this happen to some of the people I care most deeply about.

A relative of mine has chosen to live most of his life making easy choices or doing whatever feels good at the time. At every turn, "Chris" was held back by his own unwillingness to make hard decisions. If he had the option to do what was right versus doing what felt good, he would go with his feelings. He sought pleasure and rebelled against any authority

 Success Unleashed: Mastering Your Life's Purpose

that tried to point him in the right direction. His decisions would often result in fist fights. Ultimately, this led to drug and alcohol abuse, a series of women, a broken marriage and several arrests. His habits became obstacles of his own making, and his life has been extremely difficult because of it.

When you apply the BIAS mindset to your daily life, you will start to discover that new opportunities present themselves. You will feel better about yourself. You will feel accomplished as you drive toward your goals. As you act on them, you will achieve milestones which give you feelings of accomplishment and satisfaction. You will want to continue, and you will eventually fall into a rhythm of success.

The more you accomplish, the more you will have to fall back on when times get tough. The people who told you that you'd never achieve your goals will look at your success and wonder how you got there. This will give you the opportunity to lift them up so they can reach their goals just like you did.

In John Maxwell's book, *21 Irrefutable Laws of Leadership,* law 16 is The Law of Big Mo, which is all about momentum. Every victory on your journey toward success helps you develop momentum that will aid you in the realization of bigger milestones and eventually your purpose. When you have a victory, don't stop to celebrate for very long. Don't allow your old mentality to get in the way of what you want to become. Keep going. Use the feeling of satisfaction you just experienced to drive you toward your next milestone, your next success, your victory.

This requires action, so why not get started now? As Mel Robbins says, count backward from 5 to 1, then *go!* Don't think, just go. You know what needs to be done. If you have a clear enough goal, you know what your next step must be, so act. Do what you need to do and take the next step.

Conversely, if you find yourself in a rut, you may have suffered multiple losses in a row. Whatever your momentum, it becomes difficult to turn around if you find yourself in a place where it feels like nothing is going your way. It is crucial to take small actions you know you can do easily to reverse the negative momentum. The small victories will interrupt the negatives and help you win more readily as you resume larger tasks. Small wins boost confidence, create a positive mental attitude and allow us to rebuild positive momentum.

Occasionally, setbacks will happen. This is natural and normal, and it is perfectly okay. We occasionally need a reset or a rest. Setbacks give us a chance to catch up mentally to the progress we've made. Read that again.

When you successfully develop a BIAS mindset focused on your WISE goals, you will begin to see challenges and setbacks as opportunities rather than roadblocks. These could be your mind's way of telling you to take a small break. Once you have rested, resume working on your goals with renewed vigor and vitality. You will be amazed at your speed and progress after that reset period.

These reset periods are not set in stone. You will be able to develop your own tempo. It is important to give yourself a chance to build positive momentum, then ride it as far as it will take you before you stop for a break. For example, I regularly go for weeks or months before experiencing a setback that causes me to take a break. My average is about once a month, but at times I have extended it to nearly three months.

Keep facing your fears and acting boldly. Take the next steps toward your success. There will come a time when everything you try appears to fail. That is your body and mind telling you to stop. It's okay to listen. However, if you do not push your limits and find ways to succeed at the beginning, you will find it difficult to develop the habits you need to see your goals through to completion. This is a fine balance. If you have doubts on the correct choice, choose action.

This is likely to feel unnatural at first. It is going to be challenging. In the beginning you will face many fears. Taking action may even cause you stress. Don't give up. Remember, you are worth the effort. Your dreams and passions are worth your energy. This is your purpose in life, and you will discover things about yourself along this journey which give you a sense of pride and fulfillment. The challenge is worth the effort. If you adopt Jerry Rice's mentality by doing things other people won't do, you will eventually be able to do things other people can't.

Chapter 10
Opportunity

*"If a window of opportunity appears,
don't pull down the shade."*

—Tom Peters

I am amazed at life's little quirks. When you present a specific situation to two different people, one may not see anything special about it, but the other will find a way to turn it into the opportunity of a lifetime. In the 1960s, a struggling salesman seized the opportunity of a lifetime from a pair of brothers who didn't realize the potential of what they had.

Ray Kroc, then in his 50s, sold paper cups and milkshake mixers.[26] He would travel around his territory in southern California selling to different restaurants. Sales were plummeting because a competitive company was producing their products at scale, enabling them to sell for far less than Kroc's company.

---

26 en.wikipedia.org/wiki/Ray_Kroc

In the mid-'50s, Kroc sold his equipment to the restaurant owned by Richard and Maurice McDonald. Kroc was impressed with the model they had developed. It allowed them to deliver food quickly and consistently to their patrons. After observing this model for several years, Kroc negotiated with the McDonald brothers. They allowed him to franchise the concept and put up more restaurants under the McDonald's name.

The McDonald brothers had developed a revolutionary model for restaurants, but they failed to see and understand the impact it could have not only for their lives but for generations to come. Ray Kroc, who would be credited for founding the McDonald's Corporation in 1961, immediately realized how this model could change the food world. He said yes to the opportunity.

In 2022, McDonald's had approximately 40,000 stores and over 200,000 employees.[27] They have restaurants in over 100 countries and earn $24 billion in annual revenue. The franchise model Kroc envisioned changed the future for McDonald's hamburgers. It also set the stage for the fast-food revolution. As of January 2024, there were about 537,000 fast food restaurants globally.[28] Nearly 201,000 of those are in the United States.[29]

Every invention, business and innovation has started with someone seizing an opportunity. Many of those began with a thought or question such as, "I wonder what the world

---

27 www.investing.com/academy/statistics/mcdonalds-facts-and-statistics
28 www.ibisworld.com/global/number-of-businesses/global-fast-food-restaurants/1480
29 www.ibisworld.com/industry-statistics/number-of-businesses/fast-food-restaurants-united-states

would look like if we could communicate instantly with each other over long distances." That could have been the original thought which led to the telephone, cell phones and now video conferencing.

Each technological innovation started with a thought which turned into action which became a working concept. It would be built and marketed and eventually change the world in some way. Notice the second step in that process: action.

When we have ideas, we are often very quick to dismiss them, so they ultimately go nowhere. Imagine what the world would look like if more people simply acted on their ideas.

Angel investor and business expert Allen Jones was once asked about how many inventions make it to production. He supposed that nobody really knew because inventors are mostly off the radar to those who count or cover businesses but added that less than 5 percent would be realistic. Those who license their invention to a company for production probably get to market less than a third of the time.

That question was specific to the commercial industry. Imagine how many people have ideas for a manufacturing process, a musical score, books that need to be written, a message that needs to be told to the world, new sales strategies, better ways to look at IT security, etc. that never even make it onto a sheet of paper. Ideas flit through people's heads, and they spend weeks or months thinking about whatever it is but never take action. The world could look much different if more people would write down their ideas and begin taking action.

Why do so few people move on with their ideas? Accord-

 Success Unleashed: Mastering Your Life's Purpose

ing to Nayan M Hazra, "99% of individuals want to maintain their everyday routine lives with their regular routines and predictable timetables."[30] In other words, they fear change. If they were to act on an idea, regardless of its merit, they would lose the predictability of life or even expose themselves to risk.

I believe most people have great ideas regularly. If we were to truly follow our passion, we would discover great ideas popping up all the time. We could change the world we live in if we would simply act on them. Not all ideas are world-changing. In fact, many ideas fail for a variety of reasons like timing, market readiness or the number of resources available.

During my research, I discovered the prevailing reason people fail to take action on their ideas is due to fear. Earlier, we discussed the need to face fears and instill courage into our lives. The combination of courage and the willingness to act boldly will do something purely miraculous for us.

When we take heart and move despite our fears, we have the ability to observe and act on opportunities as they reveal themselves. The more focused we are on our goals and the underlying reasons for them, the more opportunities we will see. This becomes an amazing feedback loop that will allow us to reach our goals faster. We can become the Ray Kroc of our time.

In 2016, my career changed. The only way I would survive was to develop the skills necessary to function properly in a new field. In my own crash course, I feverishly read

---

30 nayanmanihazra.com/2021/10/1040

books about sales and corporate culture. I read authors like Zig Ziglar and John Maxwell among many others.

I kept seeing references to Toastmasters International. When I realized my new company had a Toastmasters club, I joined. I realized I wouldn't make it in my new career without honing my ability to speak professionally. What I didn't know, however, was that by making that choice I would see new opportunities I couldn't have imagined.

Those opportunities eventually helped me discover my purpose. It was the act of saying yes to something uncomfortable which enabled that process to begin. Because of that one choice, I discovered I could learn leadership skills, become a master communicator and apparently even an author. I developed a network outside my corporate club, and it opened the door to new jobs and better leadership exposure. I became the district director for two states and over 140 clubs. I gained the experience of leading leaders and changing the organizational culture for over 2,000 people simply because I saw the name Toastmasters in a few books and decided to check it out for myself.

Continuing that chain of opportunity, I joined a group that focuses on speaking professionally and have been blessed with three mentors. They have taken me under their wings and challenged me to develop a marketable message and to write a book about it. This was the turning point in my life.

Over the next 10 to 15 years, I will have helped tens of thousands of people get closer to their purpose or completely find it. Because of this work, more people will courageously step out of their comfort zones and experience wonderful ah-ha moments that grow them beyond their expectations.

       Success Unleashed: Mastering Your Life's Purpose

And to think it all started with saying yes. Your story also begins with you saying yes. Give it a chance and discover the results for yourself.

In 2008, Jim Carrey starred in the movie, *Yes Man.*[31] His character, Carl Allen, was stuck in a dead-end job. He was alone because his girlfriend left him. His boss wouldn't stick up for him. His friends made fun of him. He was completely miserable. One day, his friend Peter, showed up with unbelievable enthusiasm. He told Carl about a motivational speaker guru who changed his life and dragged him to the next seminar. The message was "Say Yes" to everything no matter how big or small. In an almost hypnotic state, Carl began to practice saying yes to everything. Miraculously, opportunities began to appear everywhere. Carl's life began to change. He found a new love interest, hobbies and changed his behavior at work, which earned him a promotion. All because he said yes.

As silly as this idea seems, it really does work. I once worked for a financial services company where one of my tasks was to find new talent for the organization. I met a person whose career I would eventually follow. At the time, Gene was an 18-year-old kid working at a board game store in a local shopping mall. After a few minutes talking to him about shared interests, I asked if he would be interested in learning a new career. He said yes. He became licensed to sell the products offered by my company.

This one act of saying yes and shifting from selling board games to financial services changes Gene's life. He eventu-

---

31 w.imdb.com/title/tt1068680

ally became a corporate trainer for one of the largest banking institutions in the United States. He used this career path to learn all he could about finances and has used that knowledge to launch several companies. Now he works as an executive consultant for eCommerce companies.

Gene's courage to say yes to opportunities placed him in the inner circles of dozens of mentors and business leaders who continue to help him sharpen his skills. He is now one of the most successful people I have had the honor of knowing. It has been remarkable and humbling to watch Gene discover his purpose and passion. He calls me about once a year to thank me for taking a chance on him. Even though we've both moved on from the company we met through, he understands my decision to hire him was the best thing that ever happened to him, and he is forever grateful.

Corporate recruiters may not necessarily walk up to you in a toy store and change your life, but opportunities are always around you. As you continue diving deeper into your goals and drive closer to your purpose, you will begin to see opportunities everywhere you look. Not all of them will make you a millionaire, and they may not even cause you to change the world; but they will change you. They will help you grow, develop new understandings and give you peace and energy in life. It all starts with a small, nearly imperceivable action—saying YES.

According to Credit Donkey, nearly 80% of Americans watch television every day. "On average, the typical American views just around three hours of TV every single day, which equates to about 141 hours of TV per month, or 1,692 hours per year. That's about 15 years of your life."[32] As an extreme workaholic, I do recognize the need to have downtime from our busy lives, but 15 years of our lives spent in front of a television seems to me like an incredible waste of potential.

Imagine what your life would look like if you spent just one of those three daily hours pursuing your purpose. What would your life look like? How much happier would you be? How fulfilled would you be? Would you make more money or live in a different house or neighborhood as a result? Would your family treat you differently?

To make matters worse, TV is not the only thing vying for our attention. The average person worldwide spends 2 hours and 24 minutes on social media every day.[33] That's 4 trillion hours globally every year! According to Forbes, social media accounts for an average of 1,300 hours per year in each American life. Also, Americans spend 4.2 hours per day on mobile gaming.[34]

Given all these statistics and the amount of time sunk into entertainment outlets, think about the satisfaction you would feel by devoting just an hour a day into unlocking your purpose and unleashing your excellence. Once you discover your purpose, the opportunities will appear. You will notice how they have been there all along, but you were unable to see them.

It may be scary at first to say yes to them. Each opportunity taken will bring you new ones and prepare you for the

<hr>

32 www.creditdonkey.com/television-statistics.html
33 explodingtopics.com/blog/social-media-usage
34 www.forbes.com/sites/petersuciu/2021/06/24/americans-spent-more-than-1300-hours-on-social-media/?sh=710fe16e2547

next one that shows up at your doorstep. When you have fully identified your purpose and developed the skills and passion to pursue it with vigor, you may even notice you stop focusing on television or social media altogether because you'll be so devoted to what brings you joy.

While speaking with Gene, I never heard him talk about TV shows he had watched. I see very little from him on social media other than occasional professional updates. His devotion to his purpose and the BIAS mindset he developed on his own have put him in the inner circles of some truly extraordinary people. He may watch a little TV to unwind, and there's nothing wrong with that; but he doesn't allow that to absorb his valuable time. He is always full of energy because his work is his entertainment. He is excited about life. Are you?

- Build Your [WISE] Goals List
- Instill Courage
- Act Boldly
- Say Yes

These are the steps to developing a BIAS mindset. This process will take daily practice to become a habit, and there will be times when you do not succeed. It's okay. The more you adopt these principles to your life, the more you will discover success. The steps all work together. If done well enough, you will discover the reason you were put on this Earth and the contribution you were meant to give to those around you.

When I began writing this book, it was intended for working professionals to achieve huge goals. However, as it progressed I discovered my own passion and purpose. I have lived these BIAS mindset principles.

What can you expect next? As you continue to develop your BIAS mindset, some things will begin to change in your life. We will cover that in the next chapter.

Chapter 11
Transformation

*"In this world you're either growing or you're dying,
so get in motion and grow."*

—Lou Holtz

I had my first encounter with extremely successful people while serving in the Army. Success has always been something that has intrigued me. When presented with the opportunity to attend functions where self-made multimillionaires spoke, I couldn't pass up the opportunity to hear what they had to say. The lessons they taught did not always have an immediate impact on my life, but I took copious notes and tried to understand what they were teaching.

On one such occasion, the speaker held a question-and-answer session with the audience after his speech. He had spoken about expanding our comfort zones. Imagine three circles—small, medium and large—and overlay them on each other. The small inner circle represents your comfort zone. The medium circle represents things you can accomplish, but they make you uncomfortable. The large outer circle represents things you cannot do at all. If you continue to do things that go beyond your comfort zone, the premise is that eventually those things would be comfortable, and the small circle would grow. If you create a habit of continuously expanding your comfort zone, eventually the things in the large circle will become not only doable but more comfortable.

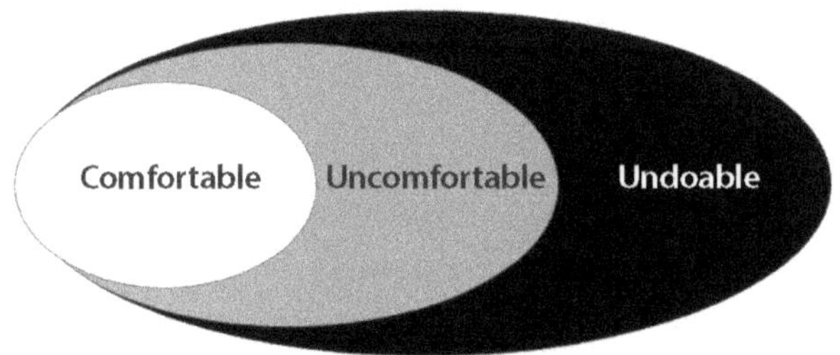

During the Q&A session I remember asking him, "After 20 years of pushing out of your comfort zone, what are the things that make you uncomfortable today?" His answer turned my world upside down. During his speech, he mentioned how most people are comfortable doing things like watching TV, going to sporting events and doing most tasks in their jobs. In other words, most people are comfortable being complacent in their daily routines. His answer to me was that he was afraid to be complacent. He had become so comfortable pushing his own limits that it was now fearful to watch so many others holding themselves back.

When you begin developing the BIAS mindset in your own life, you'll have no option but to grow your comfort zone. You will begin taking small risks, exploring difficult or uncomfortable things and succeeding along the way. Your comfort zone will grow, and you will be a better version of yourself as a result. The more success you see, the more you'll want to continue until it truly becomes a daily habit. This will cause a transformation in your life that can have both fantastic and surprising results.

Earlier, you read about my parents' work situations and mindsets. Despite being incredibly hard workers, they both remained low on the corporate ladder, a side effect of which was low income. They weren't poor, but they also never achieved any level of affluence. We couldn't afford name-brand shoes or clothing much less eat out regularly at restaurants. It conditioned me from a young age to approach life and money with a specific mindset. I never wanted to be poor. When I entered my professional life, I applied the same work ethic my parents had demonstrated. Because of that, I was able to provide for my family fairly well.

I was placed in a position where money was easier to come by. I suddenly had money in the bank and even opened a brokerage account. I'm certainly not a millionaire, but being nearly debt free and financially comfortable was a huge change in my life.

It was a very difficult transition from nearly nothing to small abundance in a short period of time. Many people who rise through the financial ranks do it gradually over time. Some are raised in affluent families who teach them how to deal with money as they grow up. In my case, this all happened within the course of a year, and I didn't know where to turn for help.

I confessed all this to my pastor. It felt strange to complain about a blessing like that. He referred me to another member of the church who'd had a very high income for years. Over lunch, I asked that gentleman for his advice. We discovered there is a difference between a sudden change in lifestyle and a gradual one. By the end of the meal my newfound friend determined my situation to be too difficult. Despite having built a business from the ground up and having a net worth over eight figures, he was unable to advise me.

You will undergo a transformation along your BIAS mindset journey. It could be sudden, or it could be gradual. My transition didn't start with money. In fact, my mental transformation happened over several decades. By the time I began to truly apply what I had learned, the money just happened. Your transformation will begin mentally, and hopefully you will be a faster learner than me. That doesn't always mean you will realize huge financial gains. If you transform suddenly and start behaving differently than what people expect, it may become a source of conflict to be aware of before it happens.

The 13th century poet, Jalāl al-Dīn Muhammad Rūmī once said, "Yesterday I was clever, so I wanted to change the world. Today I am wise, so I am changing myself." As you discover your purpose you will begin to discover a different kind of wisdom, and you will begin to change things about yourself.

Depending on your level of engagement and activity and how quickly you can pinpoint your purpose, you could start changing very quickly. This will first be seen by the people closest to you; however, unless they are in line with your change, the feedback you receive may not always be what you like. Your family may doubt you or accuse you of not being genuine. The friends you've had for years may see you in a different light, and some will choose to distance themselves from you. Others will tell you that you are doing something wrong. They may try to convince you to go back to the way things were before. As you become happier and more productive, your co-workers may resent or even try to sabotage you.

None of these events are easy or fun to experience, especially when it comes from people we love and respect the most. Few people relish the idea of being disliked by others, particularly those close to us. There are a few steps you can take that will help to either offset the negativity or turn obstacles into opportunity.

As you begin your journey, be sure to let those around you know what you discover along the way. This will give them advance notice that something about you may be changing during the upcoming months and years (or even days and weeks). Some may doubt you while others are more supportive.

I caution you not to oversell what you are doing. It's okay to be excited, but don't try to win people over to do what you are doing, because it could overwhelm them. Better to let them know you are making some changes, and only give them details if it will directly impact them. By allowing them the opportunity to watch for change, they may understand the changes in your behavior are a result of the work you are putting in.

This should not dissuade you from telling people about your goal, though. Evangelizing your goals is still a crucial element in developing WISE goals. Telling someone about your goal is not the same as going into overwhelming detail about it. It is possible you will be very excited about your new goals, especially as you begin to take steps toward their achievement. You may want to express only the high-level goal and root cause rather than every step along the way.

Another critical step is to help family and very close friends understand why you want to change. In many cases, the choices you make after WISE goal setting will cause you to make more drastic changes. These could include changing jobs or careers, moving to a different location or attending different houses of worship.

It can be very difficult to watch people close to us undergo major changes and not think they are damaging themselves. It is natural for people to want to protect us from ourselves. The more you can get their buy-in to what you are trying to accomplish, the less likely they will be to subvert your efforts.

Some people will be subversive. You must approach each of them with grace and understanding. Gain their buy-in through careful explanation of what your purpose is and how you discovered it. That will allow them to process the information ahead of time and will most likely disarm them when the change occurs. You may not get the explanation right the first time, so be gracious with yourself. It's a new exercise for you to get accustomed to.

Aside from your existing friends, family and co-workers, you might also feel the transition. Earlier, we discussed the importance of training your subconscious mind to under-stand what the new normal is supposed to look like. How-ever, the wiring will still be there from the status quo. If you experience a sudden transformation, there could be potential hardships associated with it. You will have to face your own mind and guard against self-sabotage as the new normal is established. Change can be difficult even when we expect and plan for it. Our subconscious minds want to avoid the discomfort of our new selves, and we might begin to reject it.

Our minds typically want to pull us back into old behaviors, so it is important to regularly revisit the WISE goals you have written down. Be sure to spend time thinking about what success looks like in that area. Focus specifically on why that goal was set for you in the first place. This constant mental conditioning will allow you to transition into the new you more smoothly and without self-sabotage.

Don't worry. Change doesn't happen overnight. My mental transition took over 20 years. During those decades I read hundreds of books and listened to thousands of speeches and seminars. I continuously evaluated myself to see where I aligned (or failed to align) to things I was learning. My behaviors changed gradually over time. The people in my life were not shocked at the change as they might have been if everything had happened at once. You have spent years or decades becoming who you are today, so the chances of you becoming a new man or woman overnight are very low.

It is important to be very clear on one specific point. At your core, you will still be who you are. You will mature, but you will not lose your personality. You will still enjoy many of the same activities you do today, so don't worry about having to buy a different sports team's jersey. Your behaviors will change. You will have a different outlook on life, but you will still be you at the core. Many people are afraid they will lose themselves during transition, but this will not happen. Your

 Success Unleashed: Mastering Your Life's Purpose

changes will allow you to find joy, experience the rush of excitement as you explore your purpose, and discover never-before-seen opportunities all around you.

If you are fortunate to have a purpose that leads to a higher income, there are several books available for you to read. Here are a few of my personal favorites:

- *Sudden Money: Managing a Financial Windfall* by M. Martin and Susan Bradley
- *The Psychology of Money: Timeless Lessons on Wealth, Greed, and Happiness* by Morgan Housel
- *The Total Money Makeover: A Proven Plan for Financial Fitness* by Dave Ramsey
- *Your Millionaire Mindset: A Practical guide to Increase Personal Wealth* by Napoleon Hill
- *Secrets of the Millionaire Mind: Mastering the Inner Game of Wealth* by T. Harv Eker

It's odd how money is such a touchy subject. The Bible states that the *love* of money is the root of all evil. Many people have interpreted that to mean *money* is the root of all evil. Money itself is not evil; it is simply a tool. If you become greedy or dwell on wealth or having more things, it can certainly be corruptive. Money can be used to harm others and can be the undoing of unbalanced or irresponsible people. However, in the hands of people who appreciate it, treat it with respect and focus on doing good things with it, money is a wonderful tool.

My hope for you is that you will increase your livelihood and improve the life of your family as you find your purpose. Use the extra resources to make a positive impact on the world around you.

If you happen to come into money quickly because of changes you make after reading this book, be sure to treat it responsibly. There are several steps I have followed in my own life, many of which have come from books I listed above. If you have never experienced financial stability, here are a few recommendations I have found to be effective:

First, realize there will always be setbacks. A car breaks down. The furnace in our house goes out. We lose our job. Things like this are almost always unexpected. If we are not financially prepared for them, we can have a serious hardship. It is critical you establish a very short-term fund for these moments. This should be no less than $1,000 and no more than an amount for large purchases such as a new car.

Next, pay off your debts. Dave Ramsey has helped thousands of people remove the crushing burden of debt. His Financial Peace University is regularly offered for free or a very low price throughout most US communities. There are many others, but this is the one I am most familiar with. Find what works best for you.

Once you've paid off debt, start setting money aside for short- and long-term purchases. Your personal plan will determine what these could look like. I have found that working with a brokerage can help you design and work toward these goals. It could be a college fund for your children, a new car or the down payment on your next house. This is not to be confused with your retirement fund.

Your retirement fund is exactly that. This is money that will help you live after you have stopped working and should NEVER be touched for purchases. Many companies, particularly publicly traded ones, will offer a retirement fund

 Success Unleashed: Mastering Your Life's Purpose

match. Most financial experts will advise that you fund as much as the company will match. Take the time to understand your federal and local tax laws to determine what contribution amount is right for you.

Finally, don't forget to have a little fun. Financial discipline can feel like a chore if you don't reward yourself for your hard work. Without rewarding yourself you could eventually break down and do something with your money you will regret later. I recommend you only use 10% of your income for rewards. However, find a financial consultant who can help you design a game plan that is best for you.

Chapter 12
Conclusion

"The journey of a thousand miles
begins with one step."

—Lao-tzu

According to a New York Times article published in 2018, "Only about one in four Americans strongly endorse having a clear sense of purpose and of what makes their lives meaningful."[35] Pew Resource identified 20% of respondents who cite their religious faith as the most important source of meaning in their lives. I estimate that between 5 and 10% of people have been fortunate enough to discover their individual purpose.

The BIAS mindset methodology is designed to help you discover your purpose beyond that which your faith can provide. This is not to discount faith at all. In fact, faith is the basis upon which this premise was built. From the Chris-

---

35 www.nytimes.com/2018/01/01/upshot/finding-purpose-for-a-good-life-but-also-a-healthy-one.html

tian worldview, the ultimate goal in our lives is to honor and glorify the Creator of the Universe. We have the privilege of doing that by finding and completing our life purpose.

I discovered much about myself while developing the processes in this book. My 25-year journey has taken me to some dark places. It has also led me across the paths of some truly amazing people. All these experiences and encounters have helped me grow and develop into the man I am today. They have all served to humble me. Now I can regard each person as someone through whom I can grow and who I can also help grow. We depend on one another, and I am thankful for every relationship I have developed over the years.

Developing your WISE goals is going to take effort. They are not designed to be developed alone. For example, you will gain a much deeper and richer understanding of yourself if you work with two or three people when digging into each of your goals in the 5 Whys exercise. You will discover more about your unique purpose. You may realize some of your past goals haven't brought you satisfaction because they were out of alignment with who you are meant to be. As you really dig in and do the work, you will uncover things about yourself you never knew were there. New goals will be built that satisfy your innermost needs.

A tattoo on my right wrist reads, "Enjoy the Journey." Another on my left wrist reads, "Trust the Process." The lessons we learn in life are not learned in a day. They often come with challenges and hardships along the way. As you embark on this journey, understand this is designed to work in the same way.

WISE goals will help you solidify them in your subconscious mind while learning about yourself. A BIAS mindset will help you establish the habits that will make you successful throughout your journey. This is a process. I have seen it work in my own life and in the lives of other amazing people. The process works and is worthy of your trust. With all its ups and downs, the journey is worth the ride.

I hope you are as excited as I am for your new life to begin. The excitement I felt when I discovered my purpose was like nothing I've ever experienced, and I want that for you. Recall the opening words of this book: *You are special. You are unique. You have worth. You have something to bring to this world that no one else can offer, and it's up to you to discover exactly what that is.*

You might be wondering what my goals are. While I have many goals, there are only a few WISE goals. Why not more? WISE goals are extremely ambitious. Unlike other goals, they are much more difficult to pinpoint. However, here are a few that will let you know how I operate.

Career goal

Become a chief customer officer of a major corporation.

Career goal reason

I want to maximize the impact of my efforts to employees and customers alike.

Business goal

Develop a professional speakers bureau catering to the needs of rising professional speakers around the globe.

Business goal reason

Professional speakers have tremendous messages but don't

     Success Unleashed: Mastering Your Life's Purpose

always fully understand the business aspect. Their messages need to reach their audiences without distractions or obstacles.

Personal goal

Become the world's most recognized and respected expert in helping others discover their purpose.

Personal goal reason

Every individual has a distinctive set of skills and profound purpose. Enabling them to unleash their full potential is not merely a personal triumph but a force that has the power to help them create positive change with boundless possibilities.

During the development of these goals, one thing stood out to me above everything else. My purpose is to uplift and enrich the lives of everyone I encounter, helping them to become the person they were meant to be. This is a herculean task because the world is huge.

What is your herculean task? What will you do to leave a legacy of your life to those around you? Perhaps you are like Renee, hoping to discover a cure to a disease that will earn her a Nobel prize. Maybe you are more like Gene, who's life ambition is to help businesses flourish because of the consulting he and his organization can provide.

Perhaps your life goal doesn't come with a major prize or financial reward. Like Tanya, maybe you've been gifted a unique skill that can help the lives of individuals struggling with extreme poverty or chronic disease.

Whatever your gift, it is my hope you will be able to unleash it and change your piece of the world. You have talents the likes of which I've never experienced. I can't wait to hear your story and learn how you have used the techniques in this book to enrich your life.

Now it's time to say yes to what you've learned. Instill courage as you act boldly and tackle your goals. It's time for you to find your purpose and achieve your dreams!

◇◇◇◇◇◇◇◇◇◇◇◇◇◇◇◇◇◇◇◇◇◇◇◇◇◇◇◇◇◇◇◇◇◇◇◇

Connect with the Author

JP is passionate about helping people unlock their personal power and full potential within. By discovering purpose, individuals can enrich their careers, families and communities. Businesses and community networks will also benefit by elevating their team achievement and fulfillment levels.

Bring JP to your community or business for transformative impact. Visit **thedashlegacy.net** for more information.

Speaker Info:

Acknowledgements

This book would not have been written had it not been for the support and encouragement of my mentors, coaches and family. Thank you to all who have been a key part of the successes I've experienced. You've pushed me to elevate myself, pulled me through extremely challenging times and put up with me when I though I had nothing left.

Marty, this whole adventure started when you challenged me to write my first keynote speech. I didn't feel I was ready, but you raised the bar and showed me I could do something I had only dreamed about.

David, your method of asking questions in a matter-of-fact way made me realize I was capable of so much more than I understood. Your accolades and encouragement are truly a breath of fresh air, and I never would have suspected I would be where I am today without your visionary leadership.

Rob, we've been through some deep water together. Friends like you only happen once in a lifetime, and I'm truly thankful for you. Thank you for reading the draft of this book and providing me with spectacular perspective and keeping me in check. As usual, you brought out the best of what I have to offer.

Meredith, you've been there for me in my worst moments, and you have helped me work through some of my most difficult challenges. You are one of the most inspirational women I have ever had the opportunity (and honor) to call friend. Thank you for always being there for me and always making me laugh no matter the circumstances.

Melissa, you are my best friend and my brilliant wife. You have stuck with me through some crazy adventures, and during this process you've shown me how you truly believe in what I'm trying to accomplish. I can't wait to spend the rest of my life with you because you are always my biggest cheerleader. Without you, I would probably take life way too seriously, but you always keep me laughing. I love you!

*The two most important days of your life are
the day you were born and the day you find out why.*

www.ingramcontent.com/pod-product-compliance
Lightning Source LLC
Chambersburg PA
CBHW040801120726
48005CB00012B/1258